T3-AKB-785

Abue ~ Abuela ~ Lita ~ Ajji ~ Baba ~ Babka ~ Babcia ~
Nee Maw ~ Bamma ~ Go-Go ~ Ban ~ ~ Bibi ~
Big Gram ~ Big Mama ~ Me Not ~ ~ bubbles ~
Ma ~ Cici ~ Mommom ~ Da Ma ~ Lola ~ Ma ~ Naga ~
i Nai ~ Mama ~ Mamaw ~ Mamie ~ Mammo ~ Mams ~ Maw-
w ~ Mardi ~ Marme ~ Mema ~ Meme ~ Grand-Mère ~ Memog
Memom ~ Mica ~ Mima ~ Moggee ~ Moggy ~ Momaw ~
mmers ~ Mom-Mom ~ Moome ~ Nai Nai ~ Mummica ~ Mum ~
nna ~ E-li-si ~ E-ma ~ Eena-nana ~ G-Mom ~ Nanny ~ GaGa ~
ns ~ Gammie ~ Nee Nee ~ Gammlemor ~ Gammy ~ Gigia ~
nie ~ Gee ~ Ge-Ge ~ GiGi ~ Gommie ~ Gommy ~ Grama ~ Mor-
r ~ Na'nah ~ Nagyi ~ Namma ~ Nan ~ Nana ~ G-Ma ~
nagrandma ~ Nanoo ~ Naunua ~ Nema ~ Ni Ni ~ Ninna ~
ny ~ Nona ~ Nonna ~ Nonnie ~ Nonno ~ Nonny ~ Nin Nin ~
aachan ~ Oma ~ Gogo ~ Pabby ~ Gram ~ Grammie ~

Grandmothers' Necklace

mmommie ~ Gramms ~ Gran ~ Gran Gran ~ Grandma ~ Grandma ~
ndmama ~ Grandmeir ~ Grandmomma ~ Seanmhathair ~
uma ~ Granmomma ~ Granny ~ Granny mama ~ Great Mother ~
Ya ~ Gumma ~ Kupuna wahine ~ Baachan ~ Grannie ~ Pana
fia-Yia ~ Gramma ~ Gramsy ~ Grans ~ Phar Mor ~ Grandnan
Grandmom ~ Grandmother ~ Susa ~ Granna ~ Slo-ma ~ Sweetie
Sweetums ~ Tetah ~ Tutu wahine ~ Vo-Vo ~ Lela ~ Nanna ~
agie ~ Grand-mère ~ Abue ~ Abuela ~ Lita ~ Ajji ~ Baba ~
bka ~ Babcia ~ Nee Maw ~ Bamma ~ Go-Go ~ Bana ~ Banma
Beebaw ~ Bibi ~ Big Gram ~ Big Mama ~ Me Not ~ Mim ~
bbie ~ Bubbles ~ Mo Ma ~ Cici ~ Mommom ~ Da Ma ~ Lola ~
~ Naga ~ Mai Nai ~ Mama ~ Mamaw ~ Mamie ~ Mammo ~
ms ~ Maw-Maw ~ Mardi ~ Marme ~ Mema ~ Meme ~ Grand-
re ~ Memog ~ Memom ~ Mica ~ Mima ~ Moggee ~ Moggy ~
maw ~ Mommers ~ Mom-Mom ~ Moome ~ Nai Nai ~ Mummica
Mum ~ Nanna ~ E-li-si ~ E-ma ~ Eena-nana ~ G-Mom ~ Nanny
GaGa ~ Gams ~ Gammie ~ Nee Nee ~ Gammlemor ~ Gummy ~
ia ~ Gannie ~ Gee ~ Ge-Ge ~ GiGi ~ Gommie ~ Gommy ~ Grama
Mor-Mor ~ Na'nah ~ Namaw ~ Namma ~ Nan ~ Nana ~ G-Ma
Nanagrandma ~ Nanoo ~ Naunua ~ Nema ~ Ni Ni ~ Ninna ~
ny ~ Nona ~ Nonna ~ Nonnie ~ Nonno ~ Nonny ~ Nin Nin ~
aachan ~ Oma ~ Gogo ~ Pabby ~ Gram ~ Grammie ~
mmommie ~ Gramms ~ Gran ~ Gran Gran ~ Grandma ~ Grand

Grandmothers' NECKLACE

compiled and edited by
Patricia Anne Elford

Epic Press

Belleville, Ontario, Canada

GRANDMOTHERS' NECKLACE
Copyright © 2010, Patricia Elford
Second printing, March 2010

*All Rights Reserved. No part of this publication may be reproduced,
stored in a retrieval system or transmitted in any form or by any
means—electronic, mechanical, photocopy, recording or any other—
except for brief quotations in printed reviews, without the
prior permission of the author.*

ISBN: 978-1-55452-462-4
LSI Edition: 978-1-55452-463-1

To order additional copies, visit:
www.essencebookstore.com

For more information, please contact:
Patricia Anne Elford
614 Airport Road
Pembroke, ON K8A 6W7
Phone: (613) 687-5316

Epic Press is an imprint of *Essence Publishing,* a Christian Book
Publisher dedicated to furthering the work of Christ through the written
word. For more information, contact:
20 Hanna Court, Belleville, Ontario, Canada K8P 5J2
Phone: 1-800-238-6376 • Fax: (613) 962-3055
E-mail: info@essence-publishing.com
Web site: www.essence-publishing.com

Printed in Canada
by
Epic
Press

Foreword

Stephen Lewis, when he was UN Special Envoy for HIV/AIDS in Africa, was struck by the desperate plight of the women of Africa, particularly the grandmothers who, in their 50s, 60s and even 70s, have taken on the raising of their orphaned grandchildren as they lose their own sons and daughters to AIDS. This was the impetus needed to start the Stephen Lewis Foundation, a registered charitable organization that funds grassroots efforts in sub-Saharan Africa to better the lives of the women and children there.

In 2006, on International Women's Day (March 8), the Stephen Lewis Foundation started another organization within its mandate to particularly look after the interests of the grandmothers. Grandmothers to Grandmothers was born with three major aims:

* Encourage awareness in Canada about Africa's grandmothers and their struggle to secure a hopeful and
  healthy future for generations of children orphaned
  or made vulnerable by HIV/AIDS;
* Build solidarity amongst African and Canadian grandmothers in the fight against HIV/AIDS; and

* Actively support groups of grandmothers in Africa who are dealing with the painful loss of their own children and struggling to care for AIDS orphans.

Funds provide grandmothers with much-needed assistance, for example: food, school fees and school uniforms for their grandchildren, income-generating projects, counselling and social support, and coffins to allow for a dignified burial of their loved ones.

There are now more than 200 grandmothers' groups in communities large and small across the country. Funds raised are forwarded to the Stephen Lewis Foundation which supports well over 200 projects in 14 African countries.

When Patricia Elford, a member of the Petawawa Grannies, suggested publishing this book of gems about and by grandmothers as a project for the Grandmothers to Grandmothers Campaign, I was enthusiastic. *Grandmothers' Necklace* is a book of poetry and prose, each submission a bead in the necklace that celebrates the impact and potential of grandmothers in society.

All funds raised through the sale of this book will go to the Stephen Lewis Foundation, which supports African grandmothers by putting money directly into the hands of the communities where they live, transforming lives.

Jean Ostrom
Chairperson,
Petawawa Grannies

Grandmothers' Necklace
A Collection of Gems from Professional and Non-Professional Writers

Purpose: to celebrate grandmothers and to give support to the grandmothers of sub-Saharan Africa whose children have died of AIDS and whose orphaned grandchildren are being cared for by those same determined grandmothers, regardless of their age or personal health and circumstances.

All profits from this book go to them, through the Petawawa Grannies, Grandmothers to Grandmothers Campaign of the Stephen Lewis Foundation.

It is an honour to have been entrusted with the considerable gifts of the contributors to this anthology. My particular gratitude to Jean and Byron Ostrom and to Cheryl Coates for their moral support and concrete assistance, and to my talented, ever-supportive husband, Robert, co-grandparent with me of five children. Thank you to our son, Daniel Elford, for each time he responded with technical assistance when he heard "Oh no!" from my study.

I thank God for the generosity and love that is demonstrated through the men and women who participated in this project.

The apostrophe follows the "s" in the title because "grandmothers" is plural. This necklace represents many, many grandmothers from around the world. There are numerous laughs and tender moments, but the book reflects true life. It is not all maple-syrupy sweetness and light. Read, chuckle, laugh, cry, flinch, reminisce, admire, celebrate, and gain hope for the future.

Patricia Anne Elford, B.A., M.Div.
Petawawa, Ontario, Canada, 2009

Gems to Discover

I. About Grandmothers

Abue ~ Abuela ~ Lita ~ Ajji ~ Baba ~ Babka ~ Babcia ~
e Maw ~ Bamma ~ Go-Go ~ Bana ~ Banma ~ Beebaw ~ Bibi
Big Gram ~ Big Mama ~ MeMot ~ Mim ~ Bubbie ~ Bubbles ~
Ma ~ Cici ~ Mommom ~ Da Ma ~ Lola ~ Ma ~ Maga ~
i Mai ~ Mama ~ Mamaw ~ Mamie ~ Mammo ~ Mams ~ Maw-
aw ~ Mardi ~ Marme ~ Mema ~ Meme ~ Grand-Mère ~ Memog
Memom ~ Mica ~ Mima ~ Moggee ~ Moggy ~ Momaw ~
mmers ~ Mom-Mom ~ Moome ~ Nai Nai ~ Mummica ~ Mum ~
nna ~ E-li-si ~ E-ma ~ Eena-nana ~ G-Mom ~ Nanny ~ GaGa ~
ms ~ Gammie ~ Nee Nee ~ Gammlemor ~ Gammy ~ Gigia ~
nnie ~ Gee ~ Ge-Ge ~ GiGi ~ Gommie ~ Gommy ~ Grama ~ Mor-
or ~ Na'nah ~ Namaw ~ Namma ~ Nan ~ Nana ~ G-Ma ~
nagrandma ~ Nanoo ~ Naunua ~ Nema ~ NiNi ~ Ninna ~
nny ~ Nona ~ Nonna ~ Nonnie ~ Nonno ~ Nonny ~ Nun Nun
aachan ~ Oma ~ Gogo ~ Pabby ~ Gram ~ Grammie ~
ammommie ~ Gramms ~ Gran ~ Gran Gran ~ Grandma ~
andmama ~ Grandmeir ~ Grandmomma ~ Seanmhathair ~
anna ~ Granmomma ~ Granny ~ Grannymama ~ Great Mother ~
Yia ~ Gumma ~ Kupuna wahine ~ Baachan ~ Grannie ~ Pama
Yia-Yia ~ Gramma ~ Gramsy ~ Grams ~ Phar-Mor ~ Grandnan
Grandmom ~ Grandmother ~ Sasa ~ Granna ~ Slo-ma ~ Sweetie
Sweetums ~ Tetah ~ Tutu wahine ~ Vo-Vo ~ Lela ~ Nanna ~
ugie ~ Grand-mère ~ Abue ~ Abuela ~ Lita ~ Ajji ~ Baba ~
abka ~ Babcia ~ Mee Maw ~ Bamma ~ Go-Go ~ Bana ~ Banma
Beebaw ~ Bibi ~ Big Gram ~ Big Mama ~ MeMot ~ Mim ~
ubbie ~ Bubbles ~ Mo Ma ~ Cici ~ Mommom ~ Da Ma ~ Lola ~
a ~ Maga ~ Mai Mai ~ Mama ~ Mamaw ~ Mamie ~ Mammo ~
ams ~ Maw-Maw ~ Mardi ~ Marme ~ Mema ~ Meme ~ Grand-
ère ~ Memog ~ Memom ~ Mica ~ Mima ~ Moggee ~ Moggy ~
omaw ~ Mommers ~ Mom-Mom ~ Moome ~ Nai Nai ~ Mummica
Mum ~ Nanna ~ E-li-si ~ E-ma ~ Eena-nana ~ G-Mom ~ Nanny
GaGa ~ Gams ~ Gammie ~ Nee Nee ~ Gammlemor ~ Gammy ~
gia ~ Gannie ~ Gee ~ Ge-Ge ~ GiGi ~ Gommie ~ Gommy ~ Grama
Mor-Mor ~ Na'nah ~ Namaw ~ Namma ~ Nan ~ Nana ~ G-Ma
Nanagrandma ~ Nanoo ~ Naunua ~ Nema ~ NiNi ~ Ninna ~
nny ~ Nona ~ Nonna ~ Nonnie ~ Nonno ~ Nonny ~ Nun Nun
aachan ~ Oma ~ Gogo ~ Pabby ~ Gram ~ Grammie ~
ammommie ~ Gramms ~ Gran ~ Gran Gran ~ Grandma ~ Grand

~ Abue ~ Abuela ~ Lita ~ Ajji ~ Baba ~ Babka ~ Babcia
MeeMaw ~ Bamma ~ Go-Go ~ Bana ~ Banma ~ Beebaw ~ Be
~ Big Gram ~ Big Mama ~ MeMot ~ Mim ~ Bubbie ~ Bubbles
Mo Ma ~ Cici ~ Mommom ~ Da Ma ~ Lola ~ Ma ~ Maga
MaiMai ~ Mama ~ Mamaw ~ Mamie ~ Mammo ~ Mams ~ Mau
Maw ~ Mardi ~ Marme ~ Mema ~ Meme ~ Grand-Mère ~ Mem
~ Memom ~ Mica ~ Mima ~ Moggee ~ Moggy ~ Momaw
Mommers ~ Mom-Mom ~ Moome ~ Nai Nai ~ Mummica ~ Mum
Nanna ~ E-li-si ~ E-ma ~ Eena-nana ~ G-Mom ~ Nanny ~ GaGa
Gams ~ Gammie ~ NeeNee ~ Gammlemor ~ Gammy ~ Gigia
Gannie ~ Gee ~ Ge-Ge ~ GiGi ~ Gommie ~ Gommy ~ Grama ~ Mo
Mor ~ Na'nah ~ Namaw ~ Namma ~ Nan ~ Nana ~ G-Ma
Nanagrandma ~ Nanoo ~ Naunua ~ Nema ~ NiNi ~ Ninna
Ninny ~ Nona ~ Nonna ~Nonnie ~ Nonno ~ Nonny ~ Nun Nun
Obaachan ~ Oma ~ Gogo ~ Pabby ~ Gram ~ Grammie
Grammommie ~ Gramms ~ Gran ~ Gran Gran ~ Grandma
Grandmama ~ Grandmeir ~ Grandmomma ~ Seanmhathair
Granma ~ Granmomma ~Granny ~ Grannymama ~ GreatMother
YaYa ~ Gumma ~ Kupuna wahine ~ Baachan ~ Grannie ~ Pan
~ Yia-Yia ~ Gramma ~ Gramsy ~ Grams ~ Phar-Mor ~ Grandn
~ Grandmom ~ Grandmother ~ Sasa ~ Granna ~ Slo-ma ~ Swee
~ Sweetums ~ Tetah ~ Tutu wahine ~ Vo-Vo ~ Lela ~ Nanna
Bougie ~ Grand-mère ~ Abue ~ Abuela ~ Lita ~ Ajji ~ Baba
Babka ~ Babcia ~ MeeMaw ~ Bamma ~ Go-Go ~ Bana ~ Bann
~ Beebaw ~ Bibi ~ Big Gram ~ Big Mama ~ MeMot ~ Mim
Bubbie ~ Bubbles ~ Mo Ma ~ Cici ~ Mommom ~ Da Ma ~ Lola
Ma ~ Maga ~ MaiMai ~ Mama ~ Mamaw ~ Mamie ~ Mammo
Mams ~ Maw-Maw ~ Mardi ~ Marme ~ Mema ~ Meme ~ Gran
Mère ~ Memog ~ Memom ~ Mica ~ Mima ~ Moggee ~ Moggy
Momaw ~ Mommers ~Mom-Mom ~ Moome ~ Nai Nai ~ Mummi
~ Mum ~ Nanna ~ E-li-si ~ E-ma ~ Eena-nana ~ G-Mom ~ Nan
~ GaGa ~ Gams ~ Gammie ~ NeeNee ~ Gammlemor ~ Gammy
Gigia ~ Gannie ~ Gee ~ Ge-Ge ~ GiGi ~ Gommie ~ Gommy ~ Gran
~ Mor-Mor ~ Na'nah ~ Namaw ~ Namma ~ Nan ~ Nana ~ G-M
~ Nanagrandma ~ Nanoo ~ Naunua ~ Nema ~ NiNi ~ Ninna
Ninny ~ Nona ~ Nonna ~Nonnie ~ Nonno ~ Nonny ~ Nun Nun
Obaachan ~ Oma ~ Gogo ~ Pabby ~ Gram ~ Grammie
Grammommie ~ Gramms ~ Gran ~ Gran Gran ~ Grandma ~ Gran

part one

About Grandmothers

"Behind the bare breasts of every woman lies the heart of her grandmother"

(Linda Patchett).

"From those survivors who, like my grandmother Dejanira who worked her fingers to the bone to sew clothing that she then sold on the sidewalks of Port-au-Prince to send her children to school, I learned that 'education is freedom'"

(Her Excellency the Right Honourable Michaëlle Jean, Governor General of Canada, International Women's Day, 2009, © Canada News Centre).

"My grandmother loved Pichon....I believe there is a grace has flowed down [to me]"

(Jean Vanier, founder of L'Arche, referencing Pere Pichon, a spiritual advisor to Therese de Salaberry Archer, his maternal grandmother. Charles Lewis, National Post).

Knowing You

I never knew my grandmother.
I stare at a stranger, searching her tattered photograph for connection.
You're a part of me, Baba, but I don't know you.
My father said you were kind, never argued with your husband, perfect, just like my mother.
No stories passed down save one of when a trigger-happy German soldier shot you in the hip.
A door slammed. You'd only bent over to pick up the fallen door knob.
Surviving this and more in the Old Country, living out the war until 1947.
How I missed knowing you.

© Ruth Zaryski Jackson 2009

This is about my paternal grandmother who remained in what is now Ukraine after my father immigrated in 1928 to Canada. She died in 1947. I never met her as there was no communication between the village and Canada during the war.

Bedtime

My grandmother inches her way
to the edge of the sofa to stand.
She leans forward, chest against knees,
placing freckled hands by her thighs.
She pushes herself up, and makes it onto her feet,
but she wobbles and her torso is curved, a question mark.
She straightens slowly and looks at me,
aware I've been watching, holding my breath,
and hoping she wouldn't knock her balding head
against the edge of the glass table.
She steadies herself in her walking shoes.
Years ago she smiled when I said,
"I like that you never wear grandma shoes."
She still doesn't. Not the kind little old ladies wear,
the ones with pin holes and open toes.

But she doesn't wear patent leather heels anymore,
and she's cut her hair and stopped dyeing it brown.
Polyester stretch pants have replaced silk skirts and nylons
with straight seams.
She's no longer a piano student at Juilliard
or a choral director,
or the keen-eared matriarch who, while driving, heard
every word
whispered in the back seat of her newest Cadillac.
She no longer has her leather-gloved hands on the wheel,
is no longer bargaining with merchants in Mexico
over blankets, guitar strings, and jewellery.
She isn't eating gelato in Italy, or reading my future in a

deck of playing cards.
She's not dragging me to every cathedral, museum and city
bus tour in Europe,
or reminding me not to slouch,
or suggesting I study medicine,
or kissing my cheek and declaring me scrumptious!

I take her by the elbow.
We shuffle toward the bedroom.
"I don't think of you as old," I say.
She smiles,
and for a moment
we are both young again.

© Bella Mahaya Carter

A Granddaughter's Wish

(in memory of Eileen Millon)

I wish for you blue skies
And autumn leaves.

I wish for you warm hugs
And deep laughter.

I wish for you long walks
And slow dances.

I wish for you joyous reunions
And ageless love.

I wish for you gentle breezes
And wind chimes.

I wish for you all the wonderful
Things you always wished for me.

I wish you a rich eternity.

© Alison Seay

Lovingly Knitted by Nana

My mother's mother, Helen (Nellie) Crombie, a wonderful lady, was born the youngest of thirteen children in 1900, in a fishing village in Scotland. She went "into service" at an age when today's girls are anticipating high school; yet, I think she had more general knowledge than many undergrads today.

Nana——as I called her——was an incredibly active lady, only still when sleeping. I never saw her sit without work in her hands: knitting, crocheting, needlework, or socks needing darning. The television never occupied her entirely; she was always dividing her attention.

I was all of four years old when she patiently taught me to hold a pair of knitting needles, advising, "Now Gilly, you must always have something on the go as the Devil makes work for idle hands!"

I fumbled beside her, trying to poke the needle into the loop, wind the yarn around and slip the stitch off without dropping it, all to her gentle encouragement. She would take the tangled strip from me, rip down my mess and loosely knit back up the same number of stitches she had undone, handing it back to me with the admonition to try again. How satisfying to finally complete a row and then a section of plain knitting that met with her approval! Then I was taught purl and ribbing. When I was about seven, she taught me how to turn the heel of a sock. I was so proud of that first misshapen pair. Then came the skills to do Fair-Isle patterns and fisherman knits—I knitted my way through my teens and my university years, proudly presenting my husband-to-be with an Aran pullover which he still wears thirty-odd years later.

Nana coached me through the grubby stages of hem-stitching and embroidery until I could produce acceptable linens. One favourite project I designed and stitched was the dinner cloth with the Canadian coat of arms at each end and twelve napkins, each with a provincial or territorial coat of arms, gifts for my parents.

I was the happy recipient of many of Nana's beautiful hand-knitted garments: hats, mitts, scarves, socks, sweaters and a coat. She knitted kilt socks for my Highlander husband. When I became a mother, there were the precious, delicate layettes in which, although they took time to hand wash and block, I loved to dress my babies. Nana was so delighted with her two great-grandsons that she emptied her workbasket, knitting multicoloured squares to assemble into blankets they treasured.

Nana died before my first daughter was born; however, she had already completed a lacy shawl on needles as fine as piano wire and crocheted a pink and white blanket "just in case" for the Silver Cross pram in which our children took their airings. She also left me the heritage of never being able to endure a television show or long car ride as a passenger without some work in my hands.

My own six children, boys and girls, have learned to knit at my knee, my eldest son proudly completing thirteen and a half feet of prescribed multicoloured stripes for a Dr. Who scarf when he was about twelve years old. I am the proud owner of many lovingly crafted items from children who have learned the joy of giving and receiving hand-made gifts.

© Gillian Federico

Letter to Granny Zora

Bosnia and Herzegovina, 2009

Dear Granny,

How I miss you, Granny Zora. So much has happened since you died. Who could ever know that the war would start in Sarajevo? And who could imagine that my parents would be killed by a suicide bomber while they waited in line for water?

Through those five years that I lived with you, I saw your strength, the way you took me in and raised me when you were already a grandmother. In spite of the troubles that were going on, you took me to school every day so I could learn to read and write. Thank you for staying with me when the air-strike sirens went off, and for holding me close when we hid from snipers and their bullets.

Granny, I will always cherish those years with you. You were like a mother to me. Like my father, you never got angry with me when I cried at the siren warnings. I was sad when my parents died, but you understood how I felt.

I remember my mother and how pretty she was, but you said I am just as special and pretty. When I visited with my aunts, uncles and cousins, I felt a kinship with them, but I belonged to no one but you.

I recall that night on October 20, 1995. I was twelve years old and the war was almost over. After a bomb went off and shattered lots of windows, Grandfather had replaced the broken window glass with some cloth. He covered the window so the cold air wouldn't come through.

I can't explain how I felt that night. Your house near the

Miljacka River was quiet, except for the television tuned to a local station, just low enough that we could hear it. There were no footsteps, no other voices in the house. Grandfather was sleeping in the bedroom. We sat up late and had a snack; some fruit and biscuits that we got from the Red Cross workers.

While we sat on the couch together watching television, the wood crackled and the light from the fire lit the room. Granny, I remember your breathing was so heavy. I knew something was wrong when you fought for breath. I was worried, but I asked if you took your medicine. You didn't answer. You fell into my lap and took your last breath. I freed myself from underneath you and hurried down the hall to the room where Grandpa was sleeping. It was only ten steps, but it seemed much farther. There was nothing he could do either. You were dead, just like my parents. I felt so alone, just as lonely as I was when I came to live with you.

Today is Mother's Day, a perfect time to think of you. You were like a mother to me. Granny, thank you for everything, for wonderful evenings we spent together, and for your sense of humour that kept me sane when I mourned for my mama and tata. I'll never forget you.

Happy Mother's Day,
Melina

© Theodore Oisin

Nanna

My grandmother was a classic English grandmother—pink-and-white-skinned, with bright blue eyes, her head topped with a soft cloud of white hair. She was always immaculately dressed. She wore a purple velvet hat when she traveled to Canada. She used a silver-topped ebony cane when her hips bothered her.

Nanna could whip up a meal of spring lamb, new potatoes and sweet green peas, accompanied by a sauce made from the mint growing on her kitchen window ledge. Dessert would be toffee pudding and thick double cream.

She regularly sent parcels to me, my brother and my sister. The carefully wrapped brown packages contained comics and *The Girl's Annual* and (by then) crumbled Flake bars.

She became someone real to me when she visited after my grandfather died. I didn't mind giving up my bedroom for her stay; I knew how much my mother liked her, and I was still grateful for those parcels! She was there after school. Daily, over tea and biscuits, we began to form our friendship. She taught me several things in the next few decades...

Every Moment Counts.

I stayed in her flat for a week one February, and was included in the weekly Canasta game. As she was sorting her cards, she mentioned she had no more perfume. A friend said, "May! What have you done with all those Christmas bottles?" She sheepishly admitted that she sprayed herself liberally when she went to bed, in case she died in the night, so she would at least smell nice when they found her!

Family Is Important

Nanna came to Canada almost every year till she was 98, when she told us she really didn't think she could make the trip anymore!

We Are Responsible for Our Own Lives

After her second hip replacement, a friend offered to come in to make the bed for her each day. She firmly declined, saying that if someone started making her bed for her now, they would be doing it till she died. When she was 101, after a few falls, she felt help might be useful at night, so she moved to a seniors' residence with night staff. Then, at the age of 104, she "put herself into care" in a brand-new nursing home. Nanna's children didn't have the agony of making decisions for an aging and recalcitrant parent.

Chocolate Is Essential!

On her 105th birthday, Nanna told the local newspaper that she didn't have a secret for long life, but she did feel a piece of Cadbury's milk chocolate before bed every night certainly helped. For her 106th birthday, the company sent her 106 pounds of milk chocolates. There was no better gift.

Life Is Celebrated in Stories.

When Nanna died the next year in England, my family gathered to remember her, to tell stories about her life and what she meant to each of us. There were many reminiscences, with much laughter, and—a huge chocolate cake decorated with pieces of milk chocolate.

© Judy Maddren

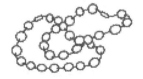

Grandmother's Mirror

I suppose it's because I'm the youngest of all the grand-children that I was the last to be informed about my grand-mother's moving into a nursing home.

"She can't take most of this with her," my dad said. "Everyone else has already picked the things they'd like to keep. You can come with me today and go through what's left before we take the rest to charity."

Her house felt extremely lonely as I walked through it. I was grateful that I still had her, my sweet, 90-year-old grandmother. Seeing her house so empty would have been nearly impossible to bear, otherwise.

She'd taken her most-loved possessions to the nursing home with her, including the lamp that had been a gift from Granddaddy years ago. She'd already given me her tea set to pass on to my daughter. My aunt had taken the cedar chest I'd loved to dig in as a child, looking for the toys Grandmother stored in there.

What on earth was I supposed to claim? Throw pillows? Knick-knacks and candles? No…I wanted something special. But everything that was left felt so ordinary.

I had nearly given up, when I made one last pass through her bedroom. There, face-down on the bookshelf, lay an antique hand mirror.

The ornate metal handle was tarnished and brown spots marred the blue surface of the back, which had faded to pale grey. The once-red roses adorning the edges held only the faintest hint of pink. I lifted the mirror and turned it around so I could peer into the glass.

Met by my own familiar reflection, I smiled at the traces

of Grandmother that I saw in my face. The lines that had been added to my skin over the years drew me closer to Grandmother in appearance, and yet reminded me of how far away my childhood memories of her had become.

"If only I could go back in time," I said to the face in the mirror as I sat on the edge of the bed. "I'd gather every precious memory before they start to fade away—"

My breath caught in my throat.

The mirror's silvery surface began to cloud, as if fog were moving across it. In wonder, I watched as the fog filled the glass and then dissipated. The glass sparkled like crystal for a moment. I tightened my grip to keep from dropping the mirror as my hand began to tremble.

Flickering like a television just switched on, the mirror's glass came to life with a moving picture. There I was, as a child, playing with the baby doll Grandmother had kept in her cedar chest. Grandmother sat in her rocker, smiling down at me with love glistening in her eyes. I realized this was the memory I had been thinking about when I'd picked up the mirror.

I continued to watch as the memories played out like home movies on the surface of the mirror. Years passed in minutes. My grip on the handle relaxed. I shifted back on the bed to lean against the headboard. Laughter and tears welled up inside me, and burst forth at the same time.

A knock at the bedroom door broke my concentration. Images in the mirror disappeared with a flash of pale light, replaced instantly by my reflection. As I wiped the tears from my cheeks, Dad pushed the door open enough to poke his head in.

"You okay in here?" he asked, and stepped into the

room. When I nodded, he walked over and sat next to me on the bed.

I clutched the mirror to my chest and smiled. "I've decided what I want to take."

"Yeah?" His eyebrows crinkled as his gaze dropped to the mirror in my hands.

"And what would that be?"

"Memories."

© Kat Heckenbach

Sails Upon a Quilted Sea

For Grandma Flora

I
On a summer's night and winter's too,
I traced the lines of sail and hull
and dreamed of sailing across the sea.

II
As you stitched the lines of sail and rigging,
were you out on the sea, with the wind at your back,
steering the ship across the waves?

III
Was this your gift to my night-time prayers,
wishing safe travel,
when you couldn't be there?

© Carolyn Wilker

Grandma Gertie's Pickled Peaches

It's the pickled peaches that make a picnic, Grandma insisted. Picasso described it thusly, "One does a whole painting for one peach and people think just the opposite—that particular peach is but a detail." For Grandma, a picnic was an excuse to feast on pickled peaches. The picnic was but a detail.

At twilight, after a sultry summer afternoon, I still long to be plopped on a fluffy quilt, sweetie within arm's reach, with my picnic basket packed with that quintessential treat, pickled peaches. Fried chicken, devilled eggs, camembert, or even sweetie: all side dishes. Peaches rule! Grandma told me so.

When I was ten, Grandma whisked me off to the orchards to pluck the succulent fruit, then showed me how to peel them and stud them with cloves. Together we'd seal the jars, wiping perspiration from our foreheads, fuzz from our fingers and juice from our lips. Then we'd wheedle the rest of the family into a picnic outing.

Despite its name, *Prunus persica*, implying a Persian origin, Grandma claimed that a friend from Hong Kong had confided that peaches originated in China, where they remain traditionally symbolic of long life and even immortality. "People at a picnic should toast with the peaches, not the wine," Grandma said. Of course, she would always set aside some of what we had picked to make Grandpa a flask or two of peach brandy.

Recently, browsing YouTube, I watched The Fifth Dimension, that scintillatingly sexy '60s group, brandish imaginary whips and rein in invisible steeds as they harmonized on Stoned Soul Picnic. When they carolled about "red yellow honey," I realized what those puzzling lyrics alluded to. Laura Nyro had to have been thinking of peaches! The stone at that picnic came from a peach, not a popular herbal refreshment of the time. Or so I love to think.

When summer starts to scald, I head for the park, toting blanket and basket, blithe, merry, and mirthful. My husband can join me, if he's so inclined...but he'd better be warned; I might be tempted to pitch a little woo. The Romans believed the peach to be Venus's prized fruit, and an aphrodisiac. Not certain Grandma knew about that!

© Theresa J. Elders

PICKLED PEACHES

Ingredients:
- 4 cups sugar
- 2 cups white vinegar
- 4 (3 inch) cinnamon sticks
- 15 whole cloves
- 4 pounds fresh peaches peeled, pitted and sliced

Directions:
1. Pour sugar and vinegar into a large saucepan. Stir to dissolve sugar. Add spices, and bring to a boil, cover and simmer for 5 minutes. Strain out the cloves and cinnamon sticks.
2. Pack peaches into hot, sterile, 1 pint jars to within 1 inch of the rim. Fill jars with syrup to within 1/2 inch from the top. Wipe rims with a clean, dry cloth, and seal with new lids and screw-bands. Process in a hot water bath for 10 minutes.
3. Cool.
4. Persuade somebody peachy keen to join you in a picnic.
5. Toast to immortality.

Toaster Faces

I'm standing in my grandmother's kitchen. I think this room of hers is my favourite. The floors, the kitchen appliances and the chrome table and chairs sparkle and smell of cleansing solvents. What really attracts me is what sits atop the fridge. It's a model of a fiery-red Ford Mustang, with four shiny whitewall tires. Apparently it runs on batteries and makes realistic sounds, but we're not allowed to touch it. The model belongs to Ronny. He's seventeen, five years older than me. Still, I have to call him Uncle Ron. He's never home, so I can't ask him to show us what it can do.

As my brother and I make funny faces in the parabolic, chrome-plated toaster, my three younger sisters scream in unison. Grandpa's playing the booger game again. He's standing in the doorway to the living room. On the tip of his index finger sits a gleaming piece of snot for all to see.

"Booger!"

He makes an evil face, with his eyes wide open and his clenched teeth flashing through a twisted smile. My sisters scream louder, running around the table. My grandfather laughs as he makes quick baby steps, pretending to give chase.

I'm amazed that my sisters haven't realized they could easily escape to the living room or just dash outside. The screen door is only a few feet from the table.

I move to the living room. There's a crunching sound when I sit on the plastic-covered sofa. All of the furniture is wrapped with a thick, clear plastic covering. Even the rust-coloured hallway carpet is covered with polyethylene.

My other brothers are sitting on the love seat, suppressing giggles as they make farting sounds by pressing and removing their exposed skin against the plastic.

Grandma sits in the sofa chair, sipping a drink. She's not crying, so I figure I should talk to her.

"Where's Uncle Ronny?"

"Don't know, but you can't play with the car."

Grandma doesn't say much, but I know she loves us. In fact, the other day she kidnapped me in the middle of the night. She couldn't sleep, and she needed to know if Ronny's old pants would fit me. It was way too late to ask my mother if I could go visit, so she snuck into our house and just scooped me away. The pants fit!

We're eating supper; from where I'm sitting I have a clear view of the red Mustang. I wish Ronny would come home for supper.

We never talk when we eat; that's mostly because we eat real fast. My father always finishes first, though. He lights a cigarette, sips loudly on his tea, picks his teeth with his match cover, and performs his supper ritual. He lifts a butt cheek and forces a loud fart. We all laugh, but I wish he'd wait 'til I'm finished eating.

There's a knock on the screen door, and we all turn to see who is there. It's a policeman. He says that Ronny's been arrested for something. Grandma goes to her room to cry. Dad and Grandpa go to the jailhouse, and the rest of us help clear the dishes. The kitchen is sparkling and smells of disinfectant. There is nobody to stop me playing with the fiery-red Ford Mustang.

© Denis Taillefer

Travel

My grandmother died with my name in her hand.

The heart attack hit at the counter of an ordinary motel café. It was an August morning; she was traveling home from a visit to family in coastal Virginia. Later that day, she would have arrived with gifts for her "grands"—plastic name-tag pins.

One year before, she and I had each taken a first plane trip. Mine was to New York with my parents, hers to Texas to see her oldest living grandchild graduate from college. I asked Grandmother if she was afraid of flying, to be so high off the ground. She said, no, she was excited to try something new. I told her I was petrified. Her flight was smooth and full of sunshine, mine plagued by storm winds, lightning, and circling of the airport before we could land. I was afraid the plane would run out of gas.

Soon after our trips, I began fifth grade. I learned of Icarus, and wrote a report on Pompeii—ordinary people caught and held forever in their last actions by volcanic ash.

My pin was red. Grandmother had just risen from breakfast, as usual, a little short of breath. With coin purse in hand, she arrived at the counter and saw the display. To the sales clerk, she praised the smoothness of the café's grits as she pulled each name from the revolving rack. She had just reached Ann with no "e," when a sharp pain took her breath, turned her lips blue, sent her body to the floor like a stone. Within minutes, medics uncurled her fingers to see the pin resting just so. "Ann."

"You didn't ask her to travel with you if you didn't mean

Grandmothers' Necklace

it," said the niece who'd accompanied her on that last trip. "Because she would say, 'just give me an hour to pack.'"

At 78, Grandmother had never learned to drive. But she was full of life, curiosity and joy. She loved going about in the world, and because of this, was what I call "sought after" as a traveling companion.

Her funeral was huge.

"I thought she would live forever," the niece said.

So did I.

I miss her, still.

I always will be uneasy in the air. But fear will not keep me at home.

Propelled by Grandmother's last mortal vision, I visit the Olympic Peninsula, Southern California, the deserts of New Mexico. I journey across oceans and continents to Hawaii, Alaska, Mexico, Peru, Germany and Ireland's west coast.

The red pin is tucked carefully into a jewellery box. Each day I travel with the love from my grandmother's heart.

© Ann Ritter

Wash Day

"Jennie! Jennie! Bring more water."
Skinny legs scramble down the slope to
the river.
My mother scoops buckets from a small
pool her brothers made for swimming.
Tears sting her eyes. No school again
today.
She struggles up the muddy incline
stepping over roots, pails biting each
small hand.

Baba Zarecka

Inside, Baba scrubs with lye soap, hands
flaming, sweat dripping.
Baba pours rinse water into a tub and
stokes the fire.
Plops clothes into boiling water, stir-
ring with a long stick.
A second rinse in bluing for the
whites.
Wring them out and hang to dry on
fences or spread out on a bit of grass.
Baba remembers…
Back in the Old Country
she worked like this at the Big House,
A girl, not much older than her Jennie.

Jennie the poet's
mother, at six

© Ruth Zaryski Jackson 2009

My Eight-Year-Old Grandmother

Our large family accepted my grandmother's eccentric behaviour and peculiar appearance. My mother and aunts often reminded us that eight-year-old Grace Griffin had set sail from England on a ship loaded with orphans. Grandma was one of approximately eighty thousand orphaned children who became Canada's little immigrants. The children needed a future, and Canada needed workers.

Grandma's first host family thought they had ordered a sturdy older girl. Their disappointment in the skinny youngster who'd never been on a farm turned to abuse. Authorities moved her to a safe home where she stayed until her marriage at 16. My grandfather, James Galbraith, a twenty-nine-year-old farmer, loved young Grace, and for fifty-five years cherished and protected her. In a letter found many years later, we read Grace's description of her life as a young wife, "Life has been kind to me. Jim is a good husband, and I am the happy mother of three little girls."

After Grandpa's death, Grandma's hermit tendencies increased. She lived only two doors down the street from us but seldom visited. On visits to her home, we knew to dress warmly. Often the temperature was set just high enough to keep the pipes from freezing. Convinced there was an all-seeing eye on the screen, she quit watching television. Grandma's wiry wild mass of grey hair was her trademark. For major events, like family weddings, someone was designated to persuade her to have her hair done.

An avid and fast walker, Grandma hiked to the post office every morning. Even on the frostiest days, her slender figure passed our living-room window like a blur. Her threadbare dresses sported patches as new dresses given by family members gathered dust in her closet. One day while sprinting past the local high school, her wild hair bobbing, she attracted the attention of my brother's wise-cracking classmate. "Hey Bill, there goes your grand-mother!" he shouted.

Bill looked at the bizarre, speed-walking old woman and admitted she really was his grandmother. We claimed her unashamedly because we saw what others couldn't—a lonely, deprived eight-year-old. She once told me, "I don't feel old, but I can tell I am by the way the young people look at me." It was more than her oldness that drew attention.

Grandma never wanted to be a bother. This charac-teristic landed her in the hospital, and she missed my wedding. Anxious to trim her lawn for the big day, she accidentally cut off the tips of three fingers. Between our ceremony and reception, my husband and I visited her bedside. As she lay with bandages on her hand and a guilty look on her face, I saw in her eyes the innocence and confusion of eight year-old Gracie Griffin.

My aunt found Grandma, at 87, clinging to a pole near the post office, disoriented and frightened. Cataracts, poor hearing and failing memory ended her walking days. She agreed to try life in a seniors' home and surprised everyone when she decided to stay.

On her 90th birthday, her five children, their spouses, twenty-two grandchildren and their spouses and numerous great-grandchildren gathered to celebrate. After the gift opening, she whispered in Mom's ear, "Mildred, I'd like to say a few words before everyone leaves." Sitting erect, knees together, legs gently angled, hands properly folded in her lap as someone long ago had taught her, Grandma said, "I'd like to thank everyone for coming today. You've made it very special. Thank you for the lovely gifts." A simple speech; coming from our eight-year-old Grandma, it was a masterpiece.

Grace Griffin Galbraith was a strange woman, the type people deliberately avoid. She died two months shy of her 100th birthday, loved and cherished to the end by a large family who understood the child in her.

© Rose McCormick Brandon

Ten-Cent Baby

My grandmother, whom my dad always referred to as Annie Doolan, was the type of woman who made you smile whenever you entered her presence. She had an almost mischievous side to her personality.

I know for sure, she had endurance. My Grandpa O'Reilly was her third husband. She had been widowed three times over, those three marriages producing a total of seven children. I believe she was still hunting for husband number four right up to the time she left this earth for those pearly gates of Heaven. I remember my father jokingly telling my grandmother that when she died, he was going to have "STILL LOOKING FOR #4" engraved on her headstone. She certainly loved her family; they loved her, and I know she loved me. I was always anxious to see her or have her come to spend the night. I knew there were no special requirements for her to love me; I merely had to be in her presence to become the light of her life.

One of my favourite childhood memories was being presented with a baby doll one Christmas that was accompanied by an entire wardrobe of hand-crocheted outfits. I later learned that because my grandmother was so financially strapped, she had walked a considerable distance in the cold to the local Salvation Army store to find a ten-cent baby doll, scrub it clean and then spent hours crocheting dresses, sweaters, booties, and bonnets for her from recycled yarn. She named her Tootles and proudly presented her to me on my fourth Christmas. Even at a young age, I sensed the great worth of this gift.

The love invested in it still pours into my life all these

years later, as every Christmas I take Tootles out of her box, close my eyes and hold her near. I feel my grandmother's limitless love, the type of love I can now lavish onto my own grandchildren. That kind of love has the capability of turning a ten-cent baby doll into a priceless treasure.

© Mary Anne K. Moran
(Anne O'Reilly's granddaughter)

Nanna's Secret

No one ever accused Grand-dad of being lazy. He worked, and he worked hard, first in the mines until his lungs started giving out, then for the town until he was old enough to draw a pension. But Grand-dad had a singular purpose, and almost every cent he earned went toward it. You see, he had a taste for whiskey, and the whiskey must have been partial to him, too. You seldom saw one without the other.

Nanna was the one who kept a roof over their heads, going out and "doing" for white folks, taking the cast-off clothing they offered her, bringing home bits and scraps from their tables to put together a meal for her Jim. And he was her Jim, even though they hadn't shared a bed in years. You see, Grand-dad always had an eye for the women, and the women…well, he'd been a fine-looking man in his day, too. Add that mix to the whiskey he was so fond of, and trouble had to catch up with him sooner or later.

Nanna grew up believing that when you married someone, it was for life. She'd made her bed and she lay in it, with Grand-dad sleeping in the next room. They stayed together, sharing a house and whatever meals he made it home for. Nanna put her faith in God, toughing it out with her Jim until the very end, keeping the coal fires burning in a tiny cabin with little or no insulation, an outhouse—one of the last remaining in town—in the back yard, no telephone, and the little bit she made cleaning other people's houses to keep it all going. Sunday mornings, she'd don her best black coat and hat, step over Grand-dad on her way out the door if he happened to be passed out in the hallway, put on a cheerful face, and catch her ride to the Baptist church uptown.

Grand-dad spent his last few months in a nursing home, with Nanna visiting him every day. At the same time, she was putting her own affairs in order, placing herself on the waiting list for a subsidized senior's apartment, packing up her few possessions, and calling on her oldest grandson, my husband, to run a few special errands for her.

Nanna may have put the bulk of her faith in God, but she'd had a backup, or several, as we discovered when we began making the rounds to credit unions, trust companies, and banks. She had at least one account in every financial institution in town, a stack of pass books more than two inches high, and over twelve thousand dollars.

"Why, Nanna?" we asked, when her assets were safely deposited in the single remaining account. "All these years, you've scrimped and saved and gone without. Why?"

Fleetingly, flashing dark eyes hinted at the beauty she must have been sixty years before. As they clouded, we saw the hurt she must have endured over and over again.

"Why? I'll tell you why. Jim gave me no comfort in all the time we were together. He earned good money, and he earned it easy. I scrubbed floors on my hands and knees to put food on his table and never got so much as a thank you in all those years. The good Lord helped me make it through, and I'll have my comfort now, thanks to Him and no other."

I guess what Grand-dad didn't know never hurt him.

© Joyce Gero

Her Charities

When I broadcasted it was true
my classmate was pregnant, Gran asked,
"But is it kind to repeat it?"

I frame her charity of the tongue.

She salvaged scraps from the cotton mill,
converted them to caps and scarves
and dispersed them in housing projects.

I frame her charity of the loom.

On holidays, we did not buy cakes or pies;
instead, the widow on the third floor
served her children ham or turkey.

I frame her charity of the food basket.

After a bitter argument, my closest pal
and I were not speaking. Gran advised,
"Swallow pride for her sake and yours."

I frame her charity of forgiveness.

Reminding me of social responsibilities,
she coaxed promises that my talents shall
be applied to the public good.

I frame her charity of service.

We dressed her diminutive frame in
blue linen, black pumps and spectacles
and lowered her into the plain pine box.

Laudable lady, Gran.

I frame her charity of humility.

© Priscilla Carr

For Marie D'Amours Cote, maternal grandmother, 1884-1980.

My Grandmother Has Laughed in Each Part of the World

A Joyful Chant

My grandmother sounds like lavender tastes,
and her hair is grey from knowing things.

My grandmother has a garden of flowers
that blooms by noon after springtime showers.

My grandmother has the tiniest hands
yet can open the jar of any jelly or jam.

She likes turnips and parsnips and carrots and beets
and has shimmery eyes but wears glasses to read.

My grandmother's favourite color is navy blue,
but she says maroon, red or turquoise would do.

When she giggles, it sounds just like a little girl,
and she says she's laughed in each part of the world.

A chuckle in Charleston, a titter in Trinidad,
flutters in Frankfurt, and some hooting in Hong Kong.
She cackled in Pakistan, prattled in Prague,
some laughing in Africa, and in France, a guffaw.
She snickered in Sydney, chortled in Chechnya,
snorted in Sudan and cracked up in the Kremlin,
and in London, she simply fell down howling.

One night, my grandmother laughed so hard that
no sound came out;
I thought it was a heart attack.

© Ray Succre

She Improves the World by Being in It

Grandma improves the world by being in it.
Each place she goes and every minute
receives her blessing of profound goodwill.
The lady moves mountains, by standing still…and firm.

She gets what she wants by giving so much
that the giving's direct: she touches, she's touched.
This is one book you can judge by its cover.
She loves the whole earth and lets everything love her.

© David C. Schwartz

Strawberry Season

i
Red-ribboned braids fall
over her shoulder
refuse to stay
back.

Grandma kneels on a skirt of yellow
rose buds   her grey hair pulled
back into a bun
hair straggling free
of pins   hair blowing free
hair brushed back
with the hand   just
like the child's.

In a clay bowl
she collects strawberries.
She draws
another between her lips.

It is her birthday.

ii
In the field, earth
curls behind plough
curls black and wet.

The strap
Daddy carries is soft
and strong
and smells
of straw and horses.

She laughs
legs sticking straight
out   she fingers the strip
of long hair running
before the mare's broad
back   and she is bigger
bigger than Grandpa
bigger even than Daddy.

iii
The hooked door
in Granny's skinny
kitchen keeps the child
from falling
into the cellar
with carrots and
apples and glass
jars of peaches and chilli sauce

but once
she felt the cellar
dark and wet
like morning grass
her stomach filling
with knots
fearing the collapse

of the whole house
into this damp pit.

iv
By standing on tip-toes
she can just reach
the handle's upward thrust.
Full buckets sprinkle grass
between well and kitchen.

Mama pours into an oval
pan on the hot stove.

In the circle of heat
she watches water grow
up the tub's sides
her moving hands
making waves   becoming

mermaid   but Mama doesn't
see beyond her mending basket.

v
Turkeys are everywhere
grey feathers dull
bodies too big for heads
red combs flopping
gobble, gobble, gobble.

Granny ties
one upside down
in the tree.   The child

sees its blood squirt
red   splattering
Granny's hand.   After
a while   it just hangs

limp.   She runs
toward low branches
branches good for climbing.
Today she does not climb.
Today she makes a nest
among bruised apples
grasping knees with hands
pulling them close
to her chest.   She
curls into a ball.

vi
She listens to Granny's
voice in the room nearby

smells cinnamon scented tea
and smouldering leaves
floating like the fog
horns over the river
beyond the street.

She sits still
knowing there'll be ice-cream
before going home.

vii
Snow overflows ditches
covers fences and the garden
path. Pine and roasting
turkey greet her
at the open doorway.

She smiles
hugs Granny and
aunts and uncles and cousins
and Grandpa will tell
stories   how he rode
a horse all the way to Niagara
and how it took four days.

Grandpa has a sword
upstairs   sometimes the child
holds it   but not today.

Pitchers of yellow milk
and bowls and bowls of every
good thing sit on the table.

Granny won a prize at the fair for
her Christmas pudding.

viii
The rope swing hangs
from the tree.   The child
pumps her legs until
she is flying   tries
to touch the sky.

She can see iris and
forsythia growing along
the shallow creek bank.

Granny sits on the step
paddling the butter
against the bowl's wooden
sides.   She drinks
the salty milk.   She sits
looking past the veranda
toward the tree's webbed shadow.

ix
There is a certain place
between the iris and creek bed
where she often plays

but today she sits on the veranda
tries not to hear the adult voices
tries not to see the empty berry bowl.

Brushing hair from her eyes
she sees Granny lying   still
near the open doorway.

Breathing chrysanthemums and lilacs
she touches Granny's speckled hand
whispers Granny goodbye.

© Kathryn MacDonald

Grandmother's Necklaces

We had a game, my grandma and I. It's been more than two decades since we last played it, so the details are hazy, but I think it was superbly simple. I know it was fantastic fun. When my family came to visit, my grandmother would produce an old brown paper bag that contained a dozen beautiful beaded necklaces. The two of us then proceeded to act out one of several variations of a scene between a jewellery store shopkeeper and a customer, until I was wearing all of the necklaces and looking like some ecstatic Mardi Gras partygoer drunk on a little girl's bliss instead of bourbon.

I don't remember when the game stopped, or why, although I imagine that I "outgrew" it. I don't remember wondering, as a kid, where the necklaces went. I did not see them again or really miss them for what feels to me like many years.

When I was twenty, my grandmother died, and suddenly all I wanted, and wanted desperately, were those colourful beaded necklaces. I ached for the artifacts of that fun. I will always be grateful that my aunt shared her mother's jewellery, that wealth of emotional inheritance, with me. Here in glass-bead form was buried treasure in a paper bag treasure chest. Of course, in reality, the bag was long gone, but it's a magical memory object in which the necklaces are always safely stored.

Some of the beads had come completely unstrung, as we all do from time to time. Some of them were hanging on together by a very thin, very, very tired thread, as we all…well, you know. But some of the necklaces were unfamiliar to me, and in a moment I experienced a realization both basic and profound: I had never known, would never know my grandma as a person, adult to adult—only as my grandma. Here were not just the props of my childhood playtime into which I infused so much sentimental value, but the accessories of a woman, a woman who was so good at keeping and caring for things that she might have worn them when she was my age.

I adore my—I hesitate here, feeling my brow furrow as I ponder whether to type "my" or "my grandmother's" beads. I realize that in the hesitation lies their significance, since they are truly both. I adore the smooth, cool, glass, the brilliant kaleidoscope they trace in my jewellery box. And part of me still gets a bit of a flutter whenever I happen upon an old brown paper bag that's so crinkled it feels like soft fabric. I don't want to minimize the jewellery game by calling it merely one of my fondest memories of my grandmother, because it is one of my fondest memories, period. And for me, the words "grandmother" and "necklace" are as close and as connected as the beads that still so often hang next to my heart.

© Mary Ann Wilson

Bougie

I did not really know my grandmother. She spoke Polish and Yiddish and not much French or English. Come to think of it, I don't know how she communicated with my father; he avowed he could speak neither of her languages. Her nickname was "Bougie," which means "candle," because she lit them every Friday night in memoriam for family murdered in the Shoah.

I was told she was born in Poland. Her passport—a green cardboard folder, dog-eared and stained, festooned with stamps and visas of places fled—had a picture of her, her patronymic, her birth date, noted as 1871, and her place of birth as Krakow.

The family story tells that she and her husband—she was his second wife—moved to Belgium, had children, and fled to Holland at the outbreak of WWI. A fourth child was born there. The family stayed until the Armistice. As was appropriate to their time and station, she and her husband left the rearing of those children to a suite of nannies.

Bougie's husband was President of the Diamond Exchange, a man highly respected for his integrity and wisdom. Bougie would have been an asset, coming from "good" family, with appropriate dowry and the accoutrements of class. Was she educated? I don't know.

In September 1939, shortly after my birth, my uncle, knowing my father was preparing to leave for America, brought my grandmother and her youngest child to our home. My uncle stayed behind in the Resistance.

Bougie endured what must have been horrific: everything we had we sold, the money used as bribes in our journey to escape before we could be sent to a concentration camp. Perhaps, after all, she did speak French; otherwise, how would she have spoken to my mother? Outward bound, we stayed in Marseille, and my parents, searching for a place comfortable enough for an elderly lady, finally found refuge in a bordello, replete with mirrors on walls and ceilings, feather boas cascading over furniture, soft pillows and luxurious beds. Our hosts were kind enough to be absent during the day so we could rest until evening, when it was our turn to disappear. Bougie thought it very nice, admired the soft mattresses, the drawings and other decorations. Clearly her proper upbringing sheltered her from understanding the purpose of her whereabouts, or the sacrifice this must have been for its inhabitants, probably, though, for a handsome price.

The early days in New York I was too small to actually witness, but I remember a fire in the building, and our leaving by the slippery cold fire escape. I don't know how my parents got Grandmother down, but surely they did because I remember a place where she and her youngest shared one room, as did my sister and I, with my parents in what should have been the living room. Crowded we were, but safe, after all.

My memories of her are so scant. There she sits, willowy, with a tumble of hair piled on her head, great round glasses slipping off her nose, a huge goitre at her throat. I am on her knees. She is bouncing me to the rhythm of a Polish rhyme which I no longer remember. Bounce, bounce, bounce and whoop over backwards and up!

She taught me some skills; in particular, how to darn a sock with an "egg" of porcelain held beneath the hole, inside the sock: in and out with the needle, mending the space so that there were no bumps. I learned to knit, European style, with the wool in the left hand. I made scarves for my dollies.

Perhaps she took me for walks, told stories, made meals. Nothing remains where memory should be. She died when I was very young—cancer, I think—and disappeared from view. The glasses that held the candles have remained.

© Frances Burton

The Dragon and the Star

A golden, green-eyed dragon and a silver, six-point star
share space on Grandma's necklace now.
More than jewellery,
objects of precious sentiment, they are visible protectors
of her person. That they draw attention to her
smooth skin and great beauty is secondary
but pleasing. Together, they clink and clank
all day in metallic conversation, like little camel bells.

Does the dragon speak of the ancient East?
of temples, dynasties or giant beasts? Does the
Star of David whisper, in awe, about religion or revelation;
of Eve's motherly, then grandmotherly transformation,
where we all live, outside the Garden of Eden?

I rather think they tell her, and each other,
about the jingle-jangle joys of everyday life.
They know much about life…about love,
about the yin of self and the yang of family;
about the tinkling intimations of oneness experienced
between and among the generations and
about the unutterable rapture of loving oneness
between a family and God.

© David C. Schwartz

Time Well Spent

"Would you like a 7-Up?"

Nanna didn't wait for my reply. As usual, the diminutive figure in the blue-and-white gingham dress turned and hobbled with great effort to the kitchen while I removed my boots and brown corduroy coat.

The familiar aroma of beef stew and onions filled the air.

I treasured these moments. Now that she was 84, I had an urgent thirst for learning more about Nanna's past—I visited her once a week on the way home from Mohawk College in Hamilton.

Sitting at her tiny ki̶̶̶̶̶̶̶̶̶̶̶̶̶̶̶̶̶̶̶̶̶̶̶̶̶̶̶̶l containers, newspapers, mai̶̶̶̶̶̶̶̶̶̶̶̶̶̶̶̶̶̶̶sed in each other's company.

"Why did you come ̶̶̶̶̶̶̶̶̶̶̶̶̶̶̶̶̶̶̶̶̶̶̶̶̶̶̶̶̶̶̶r, sipping on my 7-Up and mu̶̶̶̶̶̶̶̶̶̶̶̶̶̶̶̶̶

When she adjusted th̶̶̶̶̶̶̶̶̶̶̶̶̶̶̶̶̶̶̶̶̶̶̶̶̶̶̶̶̶, the tendrils fell gently down ̶̶̶̶̶̶̶̶̶̶̶̶̶̶̶̶̶̶̶̶̶̶̶̶̶fine hair in her crooked finge̶̶̶̶̶̶̶̶̶̶̶̶̶̶̶̶̶̶̶̶̶̶she redid her bun.

"I followed Ebby here, ̶̶̶̶̶̶̶̶̶̶̶̶̶̶̶̶̶̶̶̶̶̶̶̶

The eldest of ten children, Jessie, my Nanna, grew up in Bolton, England. Her best friend Nellie had a brother, Everest, "Ebby," who apparently constantly teased Jessie. Three years her senior, he fell in love with Nanna.

Exhausted from working in the coal mines, Ebby decided to seek employment in Canada and wanted to bring Jessie with him. Her father refused to give permission as she was only 21 at the time.

Five long years later, Ebby was finally able to pay Jessie's fare to come to Canada to be his bride.

Looking into the pools of my Nanna's dark blue eyes, I could see her reliving the excitement of travelling on the ship to Canada.

"I had a big blue hat with a big feather," she smiled. "The wind was blowing in my face." She never shared about any hardships or difficulties of the long journey. Perhaps she forgot because of her age. Perhaps she just wanted to remember the good things.

Everest and Jessie married in October 1912, shortly after she arrived in Canada. But working in the coal mines of England at a young age had taken its toll on my grandfather. He died at the age of 55 in 1938, leaving Nanna with five children, including my mom.

On each visit, suddenly, sadly, I'd be back in the present. Nanna's cuckoo clock would sing out 5 o'clock. It was time for me to go home again. Our visits ended all too soon.

I'd inhale the fragrance of her lily-of-the-valley body powder as we hugged each other goodbye and she gave me a whiskery kiss.

Once, she reached into her knitting bag and pulled out a long golden yellow woollen scarf. Weeks before, she had asked me to bring three balls of wool. Despite her failing eyesight and painfully arthritic hands, she gave me a gift of love.

I was living in Toronto when she passed away. My mom told me Nanna refused the oxygen mask when they had rushed her to the hospital after a bad fall. She was ready to meet her Saviour.

Thirty-five years later, I still hesitate to get rid of my corduroy coat with its torn pockets, or the golden scarf, filled with dropped stitches. They remind me of my Nanna's sacrificial love for me and the precious hours we spent together.

Each spring, I look forward to the scent coming from the lilies-of-the-valley in one corner of my garden.

I don't drink 7-Up anymore. It just doesn't taste the same.

© S.L. Hazell

Afternoon Tea with Grandmother

Raw silk suit, scarf, blue hair
reflect on sterling silver tea service.

Only ten, framed by the doorway,
I am awed into silence
as I await permission to enter.
Clad in hand-me-down white,
ballooned breeches, worn
rubber boots, and crookedly
pinned, tattered stock,
I futilely attempt
to brush off the morning's mud.

Invited in, I couldn't admit
I'd never drunk tea;
I accept the fine bone china cup,
say "Yes," to thick cream,
"Thank you," to two large lumps
of sugar, while I wonder
how to pocket a few
for my tired, grey pony
outside patiently munching hay.

The taste remains:
cream in my tea,
milk in my coffee,
and horses impatient
in my yard.
One day,
perhaps I, too,
will have blue hair.

© Dianna Robin Dennis

Grandmother Fired After Thirty-Five Years!

It could be a news headline, she thought bitterly! After thirty-five years...fired!

She sat at the wheel of her car, trying to collect her thoughts, anger etching her mind like the acid burning in her stomach. Blinded by panic and angry tears, she fought waves of nausea. Fired! How could it happen? Home—she'd go home and...and what? What was her future—a fifty-six-year-old grandmother—what could she possibly hope to do? Who would hire her? She had skills, lots of them, but a fat lot of good that had done after thirty-five years with the same company. Sometimes experience doesn't pay if you know more than the boss. How would she cope? Pay the bills? Keep her apartment? Fired...

At home, with a strong cup of coffee, she assessed the situation.

"I do have a lot of skills," she mused.

A few hours later, she had drafted a resumé. She reviewed it critically, a satisfied smile breaking across her face.

"I do have a lot of skills. All those years at work, all the volunteerism, all those years with creative writers' groups, all that time with community theatre...maybe things aren't so bleak after all."

A month later, after many resumés sent, a few interviews, lots of friends dropping by to lend moral support, there hadn't been a nibble at the bait she had sent out so optimistically.

"If I don't get out and do something, I'll go crazy. How can I keep myself occupied without giving up on a job?"

She had been toying with an idea for some time, and after getting the skeleton down, took it a step further, approaching the local federal prison for women about holding creative writing classes for inmates, entirely on a volunteer basis. She got approval and started the next week. The women were appreciative of her efforts, gradually gaining confidence in their writing skills, warming to her as she did to them.

Meanwhile, there were a few stints of paid employment, a fill-in here, a seasonal job there, but, at the end of the year, she was still without a steady pay cheque. Looking back on that year of imposed freedom from the work force, she prepared her Christmas letter. Personal achievements were far more numerous than she had realized.

"With the unexpected termination of my employment in November of last year I was suddenly in the unfamiliar world of skills upgrading, job searches, resumés and cover letters. It has been an interesting journey and one whose end I have not yet reached....

"...just before completion of the creative writing course, I joined the staff at the penitentiary in an administrative role for a short time. Since that time, I have continued to volunteer, assisting with the Christmas social for offenders and their families, and committing to co-chair fundraising for an anticipated performance by the Watoto Choir (orphaned African children's choir). I've also been volunteering at the local food bank since the beginning of December, an experience that has really opened my eyes to the conditions some people in the community endure on a day-to-day basis. Earlier this year, I served on the steering committee of a new organization promoting awareness and acceptance of diversity in culture, ethnicity, lifestyle, etc. To that end, a first annual Diversity Awareness Week was held early in the summer, with participation of numerous businesses, organizations and individuals. And once again I'm chairing the allocations committee for the local United Way. I expect to be reviewing funding applications for next year in a few days. During last winter and spring, I was involved as stage manager for two segments of a four-part Neil Simon play, and had one stint at front of house for another play."

She looked at her letter. "Wow! You go, Grandma!" she exulted. But how would she pay the rent?

© Jean Ostrom

Grandma's Pearls

She sat rocking,
my Mennonite "little grandma,"
her thumb rubbing the smooth hollow
it had already worn in the arm of her rocking chair—
telling again oft-repeated stories of her childhood—
siblings' work and play,
the loss of four out of ten
at different stages of life
snatched by the dreaded TB,
wisdom her parents and grandparents handed down,
joys experienced,
hurts encountered
turned into growth and understanding,
each telling—another pearl,
the cadence of her voice,
as her thumb,
wearing out a little hollow in our world
smoothing out a unique place for us to fit,
giving us roots.

Sometimes she'd sit,
a leg curled behind the one anchored
on the rung of her chair,
cradling the guitar-zither she bought
when she was seventeen,
now usually hidden
on the upper shelf of the closet,
plucking and singing,
"There was a little pussy, her name was Silver Grey,"

"Jesus, lover of my soul, let me to thy bosom fly,"
providing a melodious score for our lives,
opening the door to our wider world,
giving us wings to fly.

© Ruth Smith Meyer

Just Granny

Last summer, while driving through the Kootenays, we found the old log cabin in which Granny and Grandpa lived during the Depression years! We marvelled that the cabin, amazingly small, had survived all those years without falling down. The roof, weathered by years of unkind winters, appeared fairly solid. With its three tiny windows, this had been the dream house of Bertha and George!

Somewhere in the journey of life, Granny's dreams had been put on hold. Forcing a living from the unforgiving soil and climate meant nothing but hard work.

When I was young, it had been difficult to imagine Granny as a child, excited to receive a real doll crib made by her father for her eighth birthday. Seeing Granny through new eyes, I thought of them as Bertha and George as I stood looking at the little cabin half hidden by weeds.

Forever seeking greener pastures, she and Grandpa travelled by covered wagon over the Waterton-Glacier Pass to Northern Alberta. Delivering her son alone in the wagon while Grandpa played with the other two children, she laid the boy in an old suitcase to sleep. She must have thought about the lovely little crib her favourite doll had used!

As Granny aged, her hair turned snow white, her back bent over from hard work. Old at fifty, she became Granny to everyone and somehow her name was forgotten.

I recall thinking that Grandpa appeared extremely harsh. Although he was short on verbal appreciation, there were times when he revealed a secret admiration for Granny. He often said to a crying child, "Granny would never whine like that!" or "Granny could do that!" when one of us faltered over a task. When a neighbour friend screamed as her husband was thrown from his horse, Grandpa looked at her in disgust. "Granny would never scream like that!" Obviously womanhood was measured in terms of Granny's behaviour, although Grandpa would never admit it.

Granny took a day off once to go fishing with all the family, including grandchildren, friends, and assorted relatives. The memory of her standing on a large boulder in the middle of the foaming creek with her fishing line brings a smile to my face! She fished with the same energy that she had for everything else. Hopping nimbly from rock to rock, she finally found a spot to her liking. With a whoop that could be heard for miles, she announced that she had a fish on her line. With an enormous burst of energy, she swung it out of the water and up into the branches of a Saskatoon bush where it flopped unhappily.

At dinner that night, as a faint smile played about his moustached lips, Grandpa commented, "First damn time I ever seed a bloody fish up a bloody Saskatoon bush!"

Although open admiration was not Grandpa's way, he credited Granny with saving his life. When a stalking cougar came dangerously close, Granny carefully gave him the old Boer War rifle and helped him load it and aim.

It was a sad day for Granny when Grandpa did not come home for lunch. She had rung the cowbell loudly three times, and finally hiked up the hill to look for him. Finding him lying on the ground, still clutching the axe, she carried him home in her arms. She put him to bed tenderly, and went for help. It was too late. Granny stood looking at him as he lay in peace.

"The old devil died with his boots on, and that is what he always wanted!"

Had Grandpa been able to see her just one last time, he would have been proud. Perhaps he would have said, "I just knew Granny could do it!"

© June Powell

To the Grandmother I Never Knew

When my mother was eight years old, her young mother, Ruby Florence, died having her eighth child. As a result of that tragedy, my mother, Marion Ruby, learned only how to be a sister. Stories of Ruby, who danced around the table while serving meals, gave me insight into their happy life.

My father's mother died just before I was born and, from all the bits and snippets that reached my ears over the years, she was a no-nonsense kind of person. In the only photo I was shown, my grandmother stands in front of a tent. She is wearing a long dark skirt, a white blouse, and a large apron. She has dark hair and her arms are crossed. In her right hand is a large wooden spoon. She is definitely not amused. The photographer would have been my young dad. The tent was her kitchen.

My grandfather was an itinerant builder, and their family of four traveled to the church, barn, or school sites, in whichever prairie town he was required to be. Eliza, my grandmother, was the camp cook, and she definitely would not have had a lot of reasons to smile. Getting up before dawn in all weather to feed three meals a day to a hungry crew of carpenters would certainly not have had me singing my way through life. And all of this took place in a tent?

What basic ingredients and utensils would have made her life easier? For how many years did she perform these miracles? Where were they living through all of this? Who, you might ask, was doing all the other motherly tasks, like washing their clothes? I do know their children attended school only sporadically, and my father attained a grade-three education by age 15. I'm guessing Eliza had a right to appear grim in that photo.

Flash forward a few decades. I am married, with three children, and we are living in Europe. We are on a six-week tenting holiday through the Scandinavian countries and Russia, carrying most of the food we'll need for this little journey, plus clothing and camping gear, all in and on a Volvo station wagon.

It is evening, somewhere in Finland. Wearing a denim skirt and belted cardigan, I'm stirring our supper in front of the tent. My husband is resting inside, and the kids are likely off checking out the bathroom facilities or meeting other kids in the campground. I turn around with the big spoon in my hand, looking generally frazzled, and someone snaps my picture.

On our return to Canada, my mom comes to visit and we are looking through all the photos taken over the previous two years. Mom starts to laugh. I wonder what could be so funny. She holds up the one of me standing in front of the tent.

Then I get it—I have become my grandmother! Not the one I'd heard funny stories about, but the no-nonsense, very serious one—Eliza, described by all who knew her as a grim, pious, vigilant leader on the straight and narrow path. Caught in the photo, I do resemble her. I started to think of her, the grandmother I never knew but had dismissed as likely not worth knowing.

Eliza Bulmer Bass, this is my apology to you. You did not have an easy existence. I'd like to think that, had I known you, I'd have appreciated you for what you were—a hard-working pioneer woman who was simply doing what we all do, putting one foot in front of the other on the road of life. Thank you for being my grandmother.

© Eileen Bass Barber

My Grandmother

How I miss my grandmother. I miss her smile through her salted tears, the scent of her skin in her famous hugs. How I miss her strong but loving hands, her wisdom and sense of pride.

How I miss her—her cooking with so little to cook with; her kindness to others in helping when no one else could.

How I miss her—her attempt at keeping me safe in a world full of men, in a world filled with violence.

How I miss her—her hope and dreams for us, that we would live in a world of safety where women are treated equally.

How I miss her—her wrinkled face, each and every ripple with a story to tell.

Mostly, I miss her just for being my grandmother.

How I miss her…

© Jacinthe Payant

Grannie's Sky

I remembered Grandma as the headlights illuminated my Assistant Director nameplate in the observatory parking lot. It was a Grannie Sky. Innumerable stars and galaxies spread across the infinite black night. I stood still, immersed in time, space and memories....

After barely passing grade eleven, I'd agreed to help Grandma on her small, isolated Saskatchewan farm. The bus ride to Estevan went well, but by the time the local bus dropped me at the end of Drapo—Drapovitz—Lane, I was positive that disaster awaited.

Grandma must have been watching. As I started down her road, she hustled out, limping. I jogged along to spare her the long walk.

When we hugged, I smelled homemade bread.

"It's so good to see you, Henry," she said in the wonderful Ukrainian lilt I grew to love. "My, you've grown!"

"Good to see you too, Grannie."

"You must be tired. I vill show you to your room. Ve'll have some fresh bread and strawberry jam."

A third of a loaf remained when I put down my knife and leaned back. Life was looking a whole lot better.

There was always much to do around the farm. Once I could distinguish weeds from Grannie's plants, I weeded the garden. I supervised the chickens; she looked after the two cows. We cleaned stalls. I forked out the soiled straw; together we laid down fresh bedding.

I learned to help, unasked.

Each evening, with chores finished, we made a campfire, roasted marshmallows and talked, often staying up late.

I knew Mom had spoken with her. When would Grandma ask questions: "How is school going?" "Why aren't you studying harder?" "What are you planning to do with your life?" She never did!

Even while I worked alone, Grandma's counsel was there. "Life doesn't happen all at once. It's a long chain. Make each link strong—you won't know its relationship to the others until much later."

I wasn't looking forward to returning to the city for the new school year. Despite the work, leaving Grannie would be really difficult.

"I just love skies like this," Grannie had said. "It's like looking into eternity."

I agreed. "Let's call it a Grannie Sky."

We were sitting by glowing embers. I tended the coals while she knitted. Edgy, I poked the coals with a long dry stick and made fiery drawings in the air.

"Henry, people are like different types of wood. Some are like that stick you're waving. They attract attention but leave little behind. Some are like the firewood. They're slow to start, but once begun, the impression they leave lasts a long time."

"What kind of wood am I, Grandma?"

She looked right at me.

"I'll put it this way: You're certainly a better quality wood now than when you first arrived. Know what I mean?"

"Maybe." I knew exactly what she meant. "Would you mind if I went for a walk, just up the hill?"

She smiled. ""I'm going inside soon. Don't sprain your ankle."

"I'll be careful, Grannie."

After a quick hug, I headed for the knoll.

Her latest philosophical piece played in my head. I lay down and stared at the stars, at the basic constellations. Orion's left toe was the white giant star, Rigel. I compared it to the dim North Star Polaris on the Little Dipper's tail. "You'd expect an important star like Polaris to be brighter."

Grannie's words filtered in. "Often a small significant contribution to mankind lasts longer than some exciting invention that benefits very few."

As I headed down hill, I resolved to study harder. "Maybe I can become an astronomer, find a new star in my Grannie's Sky."

The observatory doors' rumble shattered my musings. Tonight, the telescope would scan the sky—my Grannie's Sky.

Fresh-baked bread scents teased my mind A tear dampened my cheek. I waved at the stars. "Good night, Grandma."

© Graham Ducker

A longer version of this story appeared
in the *R.D. Lawrence Commemorative Anthology*

The Day Grandmother Met the Queen

deliberately she
placed herself
before the royal carriage
before the horses stepping proud
before midmorning tea
before she thought
the act might
kill her or perhaps
just after

she held a duster
in her hand
flicked it with
a flourish as
she curtsied
clutched it to her
breast, her eyes meeting
those of
Elizabeth Rex
she staggered at
the mirrored image there
her duster fluttered to the ground as
recognition floundered between them
like a fish caught
on the wrong hook
horses snorted derision
the Queen reached down
and touched her hand

In the repetitious telling
over many years
my grandma always said she
was absolutely sure
the woman
wanted more but
"then I came to Canada"
she'd say
and sigh

© Marcia Lee Laycock

My Grandmother's Feet

I watch my grandmother soak her cracked and callused feet
in the same silver tin pail used to scrub the kitchen floor

The water is steaming—too hot
for my little hands to dip into

She lifts one foot out, crosses it over
onto a threadbare towel, dangling unevenly from her knee

The plump rim of her heel bloated and rubbery
like white craters that scrunch and bump together

She grips a blunt edged paring knife—the same one
used to carve out the spotted eyes from the supper
potatoes

Scrapes it against the now softened dead skin—
grey clumps of wet snowflakes fall away

As if she is shedding—in sequence—the layers
of brokenness and futility of the day—
the night's long, lonely hours of grief

As if—she had stuffed her pain in the crinkled pads of her
naked feet
as if—she needed to hide it from her grandchildren

I am on my knees, my grandmother's puffed and swollen
feet

tenderly cupped in my hands, pressed up and under my breast bone

I gently massage and pump blood back into the hollowed veins
again and again, I stroke and knead until the dimpled creases

Become images of the daily loaves of bread she used to bake—
a half dozen at a time

Melted butter glistening over their golden crusted tops
the aroma of fresh yeast rising from the black enamelled cook stove

The fabric of my eyelids flutters—the lashes spring open
like the quivering seam of a cocoon bursting to reveal itself

I am still cradling my grandmother's feet
a new regret stuck in my throat

My love was not enough—too distant
it denied the small comfort she ached for

Not once did I hold the edges of her sorrow
the portions that sustained her

Not once did I rub her ankles—or arches—
or caress the joints that held her up

And now I weep for a time when—
"this little piggy went to market"—

When my grandmother's healing hands—
tickled the laughter
back into my toes

© Linda Patchett

For Fifteen Cents

Grandma rode a bus to visit us
She and Mom enjoyed radio breakfast club
While cleaning clothes in a three-leg tub
Steam puffed out of a brown speckled teapot
After we refreshed birdbath water
By Dad's brick-circled gladiolas
Mom clicked sunlit picture of
Grandma with me
Me with Grandma

Later leaving at loud wrought-iron gate
Passing change for candy to buy
Again gave more than she could
Buffalo nickel plus shiny new dime
Purchased red gummy dollars
Good and Plenty
White sprinkled nonpareils
Buses belched along boulevard
Past-determined shoes tired

Today holding faded photo
Sweetly Grandma waves hi

Gray tresses, polka-dot dresses
Sad stories, fun stories
Rolling pin washer sure did rumba
One penny please
Once bought green spearmint leaves
For fifteen cents Grandma gave me all these

© Michael James Sullivan

Note: After giving up her bus fare, Grandma walked 26 blocks. This was around 1954 and Grandma was in her mid-70s. Now we get to thank our grandmas again.

My Grandmas, A & P

Grandma P didn't worry much about dirt. Sometimes you got food poisoning because nothing went to waste. I didn't like the milk that came from their two cows, but she cranked out the best ice cream and picnics with delicious fried chicken! Certain things were not negotiable: grace before meals, eating what she served, prayers on your knees before bed and not filling the tub too full. Her re-gifting was not appreciated.

I was her second granddaughter, born seven weeks after the first, M. Grandma P always took time for us, perhaps stemming from the fact that soon after their mother died, she and three sisters were turned out by the housekeeper their father married. Those girls had to eke out livings working at older sisters' lodges in Muskoka in summer and in Toronto factories in winter.

1945 was a joyful time for our grandmothers because WWII was over and their sons returned. M and I were icing on the cake—her maternal grandmother and mine grew up together and stayed close friends. All six of our grandparents are buried close to one another.

M and I spent our childhood in the same schoolroom, Sunday school class and extended family. On visits to the "farm," as we called our paternal grandparents' homestead, our time with Grandma P was mostly spent in tandem. The greatest gift in her legacy is that generosity that bonded M and me. Her generosity also taught the "waste not, want not" approach I strive for. I appreciate her more than ever; she still has tremendous influence on my life.

My maternal grandmother, A, lived a starchy lifestyle, always wearing ironed dresses, boned corsets and polished lace-ups; donning hat and gloves for her passion—flower gardening. In winter she grew myriad African violets, read gardening catalogues and prayer-book. Her home was meticulous, prescribed by the staid propriety of her upbringing. Still, she loved dogs, fancy hats, slap-stick humour and cheap perfume. Post-war, three boys overseas, a succession of her progeny lived there: my mother and I; uncles, one lost in his mind, forever in battle; another, with his English war-bride and baby; the youngest, wife and baby too (D). Grandma A had a large household of teenaged parents and three granddaughters by the time I was barely one! She wrote to many relatives and helped little girls D and me to correspond when they moved. That communication engendered the friendship we enjoy from a distance today.

Grandma A was more empathetic and tolerant of difference than anyone else I knew while growing up. On hot summer days when she'd be rocking on her front veranda after dinner (lunch), she'd invite up a passerby, an old "Indian" woman who lived at the other end of town, to rest with a cold drink. Some thought this behaviour odd, even inappropriate. "Tramps" were customarily sent to the back doors for handouts. She, however, put people on equal footing.

Her childhood was happy, but when she was to be married, she discovered her aunt was really her birth mother! The next years were difficult: losing her entire family—beloved grandmother, parents and brothers, then her first child, a girl.

I was first of Grandma A's 17 grandchildren. There was barely a day before I was 16 that I didn't visit her, staying as many nights as my mother decreed. We drank tea, watched TV and stayed up—behaviour not allowed at home. I recited her lineage, identified ancestors in photographs and articles in her china cabinet. She paid for my new Easter bonnet and gloves each spring. I ran her errands, had long hot baths in her tub and luxuriated in the warmth of her quiet home and her love for me. Grandma A, now dead for 30 years, was big-hearted. I miss her generosity every day.

© Linda Dawn Pettigrew

Our Coat

Grandma,
I snuggle warm
in your coat
as snowflakes
wind-whipped,
fly around me

with collar up
the brown fur
cuddles my
ears, neck,
my long hair
tucked inside

I remember sharing
eggs and toast on Tuesdays,
your sad face
your scowl—eating a banana
at the doctor's command

your thin body,
fingers gnarled with arthritis;
I imagine a painful challenge
to do up three buttons on your coat

frail lady
with vibrant red hair,
you endured
despite
the pain, your depression

Grandma
I never saw you
wear your coat

did it bring comfort
and warmth
to your weary bones?

wrapped in your coat
I step confidently,
draw strength
from your courage

© Tracie Klaehn

Freedom 85

Some find it not entirely coincidental that my mother went up to Glory at the exact time a power plant in our town went up in flames. Given my reputation for mischief, several have asked exactly where I was at 6 a.m. Monday. I was asleep in bed. I have a witness. My daughter has an alibi too. She was with her cousin Lena a few feet from the grandest graduation ceremony a soul could wish for: the passing of her grandmother into the presence of Jesus.

Mom had been tired of this earth for a while, and finally she'd had enough. I tried to feed her; she refused. I tried the things she tried on me to trick me into eating mashed veggies when I was a toddler. But she clenched her lips. Maybe she was dreaming of a grander feast in another land.

Then she quit drinking entirely. Quit cold turkey at 85. Monday morning in her sleep she slipped into heaven to see what Jesus was building for her. I think she was astounded. I'll bet the second person to greet her there was Dad. He probably said, "Pucker up, Bernice. Welcome Home!"

So how do you say goodbye to the first woman who ever kissed you? The one who rocked you and read to you and showed you where to find Jesus? How do you say goodbye to your biggest fan, to one of the greatest apologetics for Christianity you ever met? First you cry a lot. And then you smile, because you remember how imperfect she was.

Mom was shy on fashion sense and hated cooking. Her

second favourite kitchen activity was preparing dinner. Her favourite was banging her head against the fridge. She once tied me to the clothesline with the dog collar. I quite enjoyed sitting on the back step pondering a dog's life. But she felt so guilty she released me with a warning: "Stop running away." And I did. Mom would have been reported for such behaviour nowadays, but mothers weren't perfect back then—but they weren't absent either.

Neighbour kids of my childhood have been phoning and emailing. In our backyard they knew they could play football, baseball, and ball hockey without being threatened with live ammunition. I don't know if the decision was easy, but Mom chose children over grass. Our house was a haven. Bob Kirk used to fall asleep on our sofa. He may still be there.

One note from a friend who has wandered far from God said, "Your mother was one of the only Christians I could stand to be around." She hugged kids with more tattoos than brain cells. Perhaps it was her bad eyesight, or perhaps she had very good eyesight—so good that she only saw the stuff that mattered.

You were safe at our house. I never once heard her speak an unkind word about my papa, a preacher, or even a politician. She would defend complete idiots sometimes. Referees on Hockey Night in Canada, for instance. I guess she figured that God had shown so much grace to her, she'd better show some to others. When I looked for a bride, I wanted someone like my mom, one who wanted nothing more in this life than to follow Jesus with all her heart.

Mom suffered through the Great Depression, and she suffered through a not-so-great depression herself. In my earliest memories she is sick. I think I got into comedy to cheer her up, hoping she'd get up off the bed and walk and sing and dance like she did sometimes.

On summer vacations I watched her hand gospel tracts to leather-clad bikers, telling them the best news she knew. I was sure they would murder her—and me— but they didn't. Her charm was irresistible, even to the Hell's Angels. Mom was fearless, yet she was the first person I ever saw have a panic attack. From her I learned that our greatest saints often struggle the most. They grow saintly hanging onto Jesus with everything they've got.

With the onset of dementia, Mom's tact filter went bye-bye. "Your nose is crooked," she once told me, before slugging me in the arm. Into her eighties she still packed a wallop. "I have the FAT nurse today," she hollered, causing me to duck and wince and heads to turn. One day she whispered, "This growing old ain't for kids."

Our town lost a power generator and a great generator of power all at once. Mom prayed almost non-stop as her years increased. Three best-selling authors said they wouldn't have written a book without her encouragement. The same is true for me. Mom was a writer who was content to stay at home while her books traveled the world. She could have "secretaried," administrated, or managed a staff, but she showed me that money is a lousy substitute for the adoration of five kids and 13 grandchildren. And it was those children who stood around her bedside singing hymns past tears, thanking God for her life.

How do you say goodbye to such a girl? Maybe you don't. You say thank you. Thanks for the love and the inspiration and the memories. And thank you, Lord, that because she's with you and you're with me, we aren't so very far apart. Heaven is looking sweeter all the time.

© Phil Callaway

A longer version of this piece appears in Servant magazine, published by The Prairie Institute.

Ma Grand-mère Mélanie

Une femme fatiguée, au regard lointain qui n'a jamais arrêté de bûcher pour les siens.

La dame aux pigeons…une femme âgée, épuisée mais quand même gaie.

Trois jupes et quatre chandails portés en même temps après avoir tant souffert des années auparavant.

Tout était utilisé, des pelures de patates et os de poulet pour en faire une fracassée, rien ne serait gaspillé tellement ils en ont manqué.

À la naissance de son huitième enfant, son mari légitime ne rentre pas à la maison.

Elle ne s'inquiète pas immédiatement, par contre elle doit se faire à l'idée, il les a abandonnés.

Les corvées journalières, les factures accumulées, les plats préparés avec des produits bons marchés pas toujours de qualité, qui réussissent quand même à rassasier.

Le front recouvert de sueurs, seul, le un et demi comme demeure. Sans chauffage ni argent, la graisse de rôti comme isolant.

Les emplois aux salaires médiocres, elle les accepte sans réciproque. Les journées remplies de soucis, les nuits passées sans un vrai abri.

Elle élèvera ses p'tits sans aide, ni appui mais avec tout l'amour d'une maman. Ses enfants ont vécu des difficultés, ayant à faire face à cette pauvreté. Vêtements et nourriture limités mais elle ne les a pas abandonnés.

Une promesse se gardait-elle, des études éventuelles. C'est à l'âge de soixante-treize ans qu'elle obtiendra son diplôme d'études secondaires.

À nous, ses petits enfants elle a laissé le courage de continuer et de ne pas lâcher.

Une telle force peut être intimidante surtout pour nous qui n'avons pas connu la souffrance.

On ne peut qu'espérer avoir la force de transmettre aux nôtres ce qu'elle a su si bien inculquer.

Un seul regret pour nos enfants, c'est le fait qu'ils n'auront pas eu la chance de la connaître. Néanmoins, les récits racontés, les anecdotes répétées feront qu'elle sera toujours présente.

Dans nos cœurs, dans nos pensées, dans nos gestes quotidiens.

© Chantal Bigras

Something from Nothing

Remember the old cardboard suitcase? I believe my brother was six and I was nine that summer. We were mid-week in our vacation with you. No parents. Vacation Bible School. Tons of our favourite foods. Yet none of this abated my boredom. I was a child intent on staying busy, always moving.

"I'm bored", I whined. "I've climbed the magnolia, picked all the ripe vegetables and danced to the Andy Williams records. What else is there to do?"

Your solemn perusal told me you seriously considered both my plight and a new plan of action. With a smile, I patiently followed you from closet to cabinet, quickly intrigued by the mound of items gathering in the middle of the living room. A bedraggled bedspread; base color red, but sprinkled liberally with navy blue flowers. An assortment of tiny pots, cups, bowls and spoons. My child-sized wicker chair. And, finally, the little gray suitcase.

"Here's everything you need to go on an adventure. Take it outside and after you're done, come and tell me all about it!"

The fires of imagination burn brightly after being fueled by bedspread and suitcase: I explored the Amazon while living in my brightly colored tent, battling natives and conquering crocs! I opened a restaurant and invited my grandparents to dinner. I exhibited excellent culinary skill by serving fern leaf stew. A bit of rope and two closely located trees created the curtain that made my brother and me famous in our own variety show. Was it then I learned to sing in harmony? Somewhere I still have the hand-colored program tucked safely in a box. Imagination upon imagination swept us away that summer.

It's forty plus years later now and I finally understand where your ministrations came from. As I look into the face of my only granddaughter I know there are so many things I want to teach her. But most of all, I just want to play with her. Play like you played with me. I want to make mud pies and walk through water puddles. I want to stick crayons up my nose and laugh about being mischievous. I want to help her to make something out of nothing!

My dear and precious Gigi: thank you for always being the consistent playmate in my life who enabled me to explore the joys of childhood and beyond. I also want you to know that your legend lives on. I promise to keep the memories and the mayhem going with your great-great granddaughter.

I still love you and miss you.

Mel

© Melanie Stiles

Abue ~ Abuela ~ Lita ~ Ajji ~ Baba ~ Babka ~ Babcia ~
Maw ~ Bamma ~ Go-Go ~ Bana ~ Banma ~ Beebaw ~ Bibi
Big Gram ~ Big Mama ~ MeMot ~ Mim ~ Bubbie ~ Bubbles ~
Ma ~ Cici ~ Mommom ~ Da Ma ~ Lola ~ Ma ~ Maga ~
Mai ~ Mama ~ Mamaw ~ Mamie ~ Mammo ~ Mams ~ Maw-
w ~ Mardi ~ Marme ~ Mema ~ Meme ~ Grand-Mère ~ Memog
Memom ~ Mica ~ Mima ~ Moggee ~ Moggy ~ Momaw
mmers ~ Mom-Mom ~ Moome ~ Nai Nai ~ Mummica ~ Mum
nna ~ E-li-si ~ E-ma ~ Eena-nana ~ G-Mom ~ Nanny ~ GaGa
ns ~ Gammie ~ NeeNee ~ Gammlemor ~ Gammy ~ Gigia
nie ~ Gee ~ Ge-Ge ~ GiGi ~ Gommie ~ Gommy ~ Grama ~ Mor-
r ~ Na'nah ~ Namaw ~ Namma ~ Nan ~ Nana ~ G-Ma
nagrandma ~ Nanoo ~ Naunua ~ Nema ~ NiNi ~ Ninna ~
ny ~ Nona ~ Nonna ~ Nonnie ~ Nonno ~ Nonny ~ NunNun ~
aachan ~ Oma ~ Gogo ~ Pabby ~ Gram ~ Grammie ~
mmommie ~ Gramms ~ Gran ~ Gran Gran ~ Grandma ~
ndmama ~ Grandneir ~ Grandmomma ~ Seanmhathair
nma ~ Granmomma ~ Granny ~ Grannymama ~ GreatMother ~
Ya ~ Gumma ~ Kupuna wahine ~ Baachan ~ Grannie ~ Pama
Yia-Yia ~ Gramma ~ Gramsy ~ Grams ~ Phar-Mor ~ Grandnan
randmom ~ Grandmother ~ Sasa ~ Granna ~ Slo-ma ~ Sweetie
Sweetums ~ Tetah ~ Tutu wahine ~ Vo-Vo ~ Lela ~ Nanna ~
ugie ~ Grand-mère ~ Abue ~ Abuela ~ Lita ~ Ajji ~ Baba ~
abka ~ Babcia ~ MeeMaw ~ Bamma ~ Go-Go ~ Bana ~ Banma
Beebaw ~ Bibi ~ Big Gram ~ Big Mama ~ MeMot ~ Mim ~
bbie ~ Bubbles ~ Mo Ma ~ Cici ~ Mommom ~ Da Ma ~ Lola ~
a ~ Maga ~ MaiMai ~ Mama ~ Mamaw ~ Mamie ~ Mammo ~
ums ~ Maw-Maw ~ Mardi ~ Marme ~ Mema ~ Meme ~ Grand-
re ~ Memog ~ Memom ~ Mica ~ Mima ~ Moggee ~ Moggy ~
maw ~ Mommers ~ Mom-Mom ~ Moome ~ Nai Nai ~ Mummica
Mum ~ Nanna ~ E-li-si ~ E-ma ~ Eena-nana ~ G-Mom ~ Nanny
GaGa ~ Gams ~ Gammie ~ NeeNee ~ Gammlemor ~ Gammy ~
gia ~ Gannie ~ Gee ~ Ge-Ge ~ GiGi ~ Gommie ~ Gommy ~ Grama
Mor-Mor ~ Na'nah ~ Namaw ~ Namma ~ Nan ~ Nana ~ G-Ma
Nanagrandma ~ Nanoo ~ Naunua ~ Nema ~ NiNi ~ Ninna ~
nny ~ Nona ~ Nonna ~ Nonnie ~ Nonno ~ Nonny ~ NunNun ~
aachan ~ Oma ~ Gogo ~ Pabby ~ Gram ~ Grammie ~
mmommie ~ Gramms ~ Gran ~ Gran Gran ~ Grandma ~ Grand

~ Abue ~ Abuela ~ Lita ~ Ajji ~ Baba ~ Babka ~ Babci
MeeMaw ~ Bamma ~ Go-Go ~ Bana ~ Banma ~ Beebaw ~ B
~ Big Gram ~ Big Mama ~ MeMot ~ Mim ~ Bubbie ~ Bubble
Mo Ma ~ Cici ~ Mommom ~ Da Ma ~ Lola ~ Ma ~ Maga
MaiMai ~ Mama ~ Mamaw ~ Mamie ~ Mammo ~ Mams ~ Ma
Maw ~ Mardi ~ Marme ~ Mema ~ Meme ~ Grand-Mère ~ Mer
~ Memom ~ Mica ~ Mima ~ Moggee ~ Moggy ~ Momau
Mommers ~ Mom-Mom ~ Moome ~ Nai Nai ~ Mummica ~ Mu
Nanna ~ E-li-si ~ E-ma ~ Eena-nana ~ G-Mom ~ Nanny ~ GaG
Gams ~ Gammie ~ NeeNee ~ Gammlemor ~ Gammy ~ Gigia
Gannie ~ Gee ~ Ge-Ge ~ GiGi ~ Gommie ~ Gommy ~ Grama ~ M
Mor ~ Na'nah ~ Namaw ~ Namma ~ Nan ~ Nana ~ G-Me
Nanagrandma ~ Nanoo ~ Naunua ~ Nema ~ NiNi ~ Ninne
Ninny ~ Nona ~ Nonna ~ Nonnie ~ Nonno ~ Nonny ~ Nun Na
Obaachan ~ Oma ~ Gogo ~ Pabby ~ Gram ~ Grammie
Grammommie ~ Gramms ~ Gran ~ Gran Gran ~ Grandma
Grandmama ~ Grandmeir ~ Grandmomma ~ Seanmhathair
Granma ~ Granmomma ~Granny ~ Grannymama ~ Great Mothe
YaYa ~ Gumma ~ Kupuna wahine ~ Baachan ~ Grannie ~ Pa
~ Yia-Yia ~ Gramma ~ Gramsy ~ Grams ~ Phar-Mor ~ Grandr
~ Grandmom ~ Grandmother ~ Sasa ~ Granna ~ Slo-ma ~ Swee
~ Sweetums ~ Tetah ~ Tutu wahine ~ Vo-Vo ~ Lela ~ Nanne
Bougie ~ Grand-mère ~ Abue ~ Abuela ~ Lita ~ Ajji ~ Babe
Babka ~ Babcia ~ MeeMaw ~ Bamma ~ Go-Go ~ Bana ~ Ban
~ Beebaw ~ Bibi ~ Big Gram ~ Big Mama ~ MeMot ~ Min
Bubbie ~ Bubbles ~ Mo Ma ~ Cici ~ Mommom ~ Da Ma ~ Lole
Ma ~ Maga ~ MaiMai ~ Mama ~ Mamaw ~ Mamie ~ Mammo
Mams ~ Maw-Maw ~ Mardi ~ Marme ~ Mema ~ Meme ~ Gran
Mère ~ Memog ~ Memom ~ Mica ~ Mima ~ Moggee ~ Moggy
Momaw ~ Mommers ~ Mom-Mom ~ Moome ~ Nai Nai ~ Mumm
~ Mum ~ Nanna ~ E-li-si ~ E-ma ~ Eena-nana ~ G-Mom ~ Nan
~ GaGa ~ Gams ~ Gammie ~ NeeNee ~ Gammlemor ~ Gammy
Gigia ~ Gannie ~ Gee ~ Ge-Ge ~ GiGi ~ Gommie ~ Gommy ~ Grai
~ Mor-Mor ~ Na'nah ~ Namaw ~ Namma ~ Nan ~ Nana ~ G-
~ Nanagrandma ~ Nanoo ~ Naunua ~ Nema ~ NiNi ~ Ninna
Ninny ~ Nona ~ Nonna ~Nonnie ~ Nonno ~ Nonny ~ Nun Nu
Obaachan ~ Oma ~ Gogo ~ Pabby ~ Gram ~ Grammie
Grammommie ~ Gramms ~ Gran ~ Gran Gran ~ Grandma ~ Gra

part two

Being a Grandmother

"I really want to be a good Gram"

(Cheryl Coates).

"Isn't it wonderful that grand-parenting allows us a second chance?"

(Heather Campbell).

"Taking grandchildren shopping is like taking a fox on a tour of a chicken house"

(Fern Boldt).

Grandmother Undefined

There are few memories of one grandmother,
none of the other.
I can only yearn or ponder.
I might go by the traits of my mother.

I'll polish my views, learn as much as I can,
make sure I get it right;
I want to be a good Gram.

© Cheryl Coates

My First Grandchild

I'd thought, "It's never going to be. I must not hope to be
a grandma;
Too many reasons why my three will not conceive."

"Dear Lord, I heard the wondrous news. My son will soon
become a dad."

God gives good gifts to those who love and wait for him.

Because of science's advance, I gaze upon a picture of the
precious child.
The first image, I hope, of many more.

"May God protect your mom from harm
And keep you safe within her womb.
Child of love,
Soon I will hold you in my eager arms."

© Heather Kendall

It's All Hard

I am 46 and have 12 grandchildren.

I had eight children of my own. Two have died. I look after two of my grandchildren. Aristide Domingos Macamo is six, and he is my daughter's son. She gave birth to him when she was 17 and died two months later. I don't know what she died of. She coughed and coughed and seemed to lose all her strength immediately after she had the baby. When she got sick, her husband disappeared.

I also look after a four-year-old grandchild, the son of my other daughter. She is 20 and already divorced. She just disappeared and left her son behind.

One of the most difficult things is finding money for the school. We have to help pay for the guards at the school. Why do we have guards? It's necessary, otherwise street kids will break in and steal everything—they steal the schoolchildren's bags and shoes. I can't say what the hardest part of my life is because it's all hard.

Avelina Fehias Mahungne—sub-Saharan African grandmother

Quoted in *The Ottawa Citizen* © CanWest MediaWorks
Publications Inc.

The Pooping Success

My Nonnie was my favourite grandma, and I asked that I be called that when my first grandchild was born. To my delight, I got a call the other day. "Nonnie," my daughter's tiny voice, struggling not to laugh, said, "I rolled over by missef today!!"

"Oh, BabyJordan," I exclaimed. "It is much too early to be doing that!"

"Yes, Nonnie, I am advanced."

Sweet child. All I have to do is think of her and I am happy.

My husband called our youngest daughter BabyJacqueline for months after she was born, saying it as one word. Now, BabyJordan comes easily to my tongue when I speak about our first grandchild. Jordan's mother is a quiet beauty, a spiritual and gracious woman, and her father is an intense, handsome, and intelligent man. BabyJordan constantly has visitors to cuddle and praise her. This child has brought us all closer together. For that I am grateful. She will do well in this family filled with love.

That household's first baby is Hope, a gangly dog who never seems to lose his "puppiness." On my visits, I find Hope much subdued in the back yard, so each morning I take Jordan out back and throw Hope's balls across the yard for her to fetch. Out comes Hope's playfulness again. She doesn't seem to mind at all that I have her rival in my arms.

When we tire of the game, I sit under a shade tree with BabyJordan on my lap and Hope at my side. I sing, talk to them or just daydream. I can't remember being so still for so long.

Back inside, I do a thorough cleaning of their home while Jordan naps in her swing, as that is what Nonnies do when new babies arrive. I go to the store and run other errands and do lots of cooking for the freezer.

One day, I took Jordan by myself to visit our cousins. Of course, nowadays the baby has to ride in the back and we check on her by a little mirror attached above her car seat. My arm is bruised where I continually stretched to hold the bottle or find a toy. She hates to be ignored, so I made many stops just to hold and cuddle her and give her some of Mommy's milk that had filled three bottles for the day. Then we made some more stops to change the wet diapers in which she hates to sit. It was a very long day.

Coming home, we had to call Mommy to meet us with more milk (in the real thing) because we just weren't going to make it. Nonnie and Mommy got to stop for Mexican food since we were out and that was special.

Speaking of food, Mommy had mentioned that Jordan, as a breast-fed baby, often went more than a week before she pooped. She was getting worried and thought it might have something to do with how well Mommy was eating.

I was fixing home-cooked meals while I was there. On the second day, Jordan started pooping and kept pooping and pooping. It was a pooping success! Even after I returned home, she continued to poop regularly and I received phone calls each time it happened! It was the highlight of my day. I never had to say a word! Nonnie's success had taught the dietary lesson.

© Janet "Nonnie" LaPlante

Grandkids Say the Darndest Things

I am now the proud grandma of four, two of them early Christmas presents last year. I look forward to what these little jewels will bring into my life.

Art Linkletter said, "Children say the darndest things." I think he really meant "grandchildren"! Charleigh, who lives closest to us, comes more often for sleepovers. When she was younger, she would call out in the morning for our attention. Now, at six years, going on thirty, when she awakes, she putters around her room, making the bed, reading, or getting dressed, in other words, letting Granny sleep a little longer. Then she will come into our room.

One morning, she must have stared at me for a few moments before waking me with these words, "Granny, you're old! Old people die"—certainly not that which I wanted to hear first thing in the morning.

Charleigh welcomed her new sister, Chloe, with affection. Fortunately, most people who came to visit and fuss over Chloe brought something special for Charleigh. She maintained her equanimity for about one week after Chloe came home. That night, her mother went out to shop, leaving Daddy in charge. Chloe woke up and grew increasingly stressed that her only source of food, with its comfort and warmth, was not responding to her cries. Her cries grew louder and more frantic. Covering her ears Charleigh shouted at her father, "I don't think I can stand this. It's not what I expected!"

My grandson Justin is equally forthright when something needs to be said. At Christmas he received a card from my daughter and her family. Inside the card was an IOU for a very special computer game. Not knowing that, Justin opened the card, looked inside, then looked up, frowning, and declared, "This is what I get—a card?!" The adults just burst out laughing.

I treasure what my grandchildren have to say. What I like most is the easy way they say, "I love you, Granny." It sure makes this "old lady" feel wonderful.

© L. June Stevenson

Tea Party

For Elizabeth

A dazzling welcome from the backseat of your mother's car—little legs kicking up and down and your breathtaking smile.

You gather a bouquet of dandelions for our luncheon.

Like a mother with cubs, you draw together "Bunny-Bear," Charlie and Toni in baby carriages and wheel them to your elaborately set table. Jade, your sea-turtle, cannot make it and Pierre, your piggy, is upstate.

You serve pizza-cake made from wooden blocks, pour apple-blossom tea into dainty pink cups, then sit down next to me.

The grass is profoundly greener on my side of the street.

© Martha Deborah Hall

Note: Read a slightly different version of this poem in the poet's recently released book, *My Side of the Street*, Plain View Press.

Grandmothers' Necklace

The "Homecoming"

"What happened to your hair, Grandma?" Trenton asked as he rubbed his chubby fingers over my fuzzy head.

"Do you mean why does my head feel funny?"

I hugged my sweetheart grandson a little closer.

My locks and even a few eyebrows and lashes are starting to make an appearance now that my chemotherapy treatments are finished, thank goodness. At first, getting used to being hairless was a bit of a stretch for this vain old gal.

Eventually, though, I got used to it and I really don't mind going without a hat, even in public now. I definitely never wear any chapeau of any description within my own walls. Too hot. Too bothersome. Too indicative that vanity still gnaws.

It's been almost six months since my locks departed. That's a significant portion of three-year-old Trenton's life when I think about it. Grandma without hair has been the norm for a while. So as he ran his little fingers along the top of my head yesterday, Trenton got a bit of a surprise.

"Grandma's hair is starting to grow back," I told the little munchkin.

Trenton looked at me with that irresistible grin and then stroked my head once again and made the most precious statement: "Grandma. Your hair is coming back home!"

So there I have it. My hair as it slowly emerges really is coming home to roost—right on top of my head. And for that I am grateful. I'm not particularly fond of the hue, however, but I keep telling myself—at least it's hair.

I remember when Trenton asked me what had happened to my hair when I lost it as a result of the chemotherapy back in June. I wrote a poem for Trenton entitled "Where is Grandma's Hair?"

Here's a taste:

Where is Grandma's Hair?

I looked in the bathroom
I looked behind the chair
I looked in the cupboard
Where is Grandma's hair?

I looked in my bedroom
I looked in my bed
I'm worried about Grandma—
There's no hair on her head.

I called up the doctor
On my plastic phone
But he would not answer
There was no dial tone.

I looked in the laundry room
I looked on the shelf
I looked in the basket
I could not find it myself.

So I went up to Mommy
And asked her what was wrong
"Grandma's hair has disappeared—
It used to be so long."

"Grandma has a sickness,"
Mommy's face looked sad.
"The doctor called it cancer
But the news isn't bad."

"When Grandma went to hospital
The doctor said, 'Don't fret.'
We'll give her some medicine
No need to be upset."

I went into Grandma's room
She was wearing a hat
She gave me a hug and asked,
"Shall we have a chat?"

"Yes," I told my Grandma
"Where is your hair?
I have looked in every room
I even said a prayer."

"The medicine the doctor gives,
Sometimes makes me sick,
My hair fell out" but then she said,
"It will soon grow back in thick."

Then Grandma told me something else
She said, "Come over here."
She winked and opened up a drawer
And then she pulled me near.

I did not need to search again
For Grandma's long, lost hair.

When I looked inside the drawer
I laughed at what was there.

Grandma called them "hair hats"
Blonde, black, brown and red
Wigs of every size and shape
To cover her bald head!

© Glynis M. Belec

Grandmothers' Necklace

Not My Way to Sit with My Arms Crossed

I am 53 and have six grandchildren between 12 and 14.

Three are from my son who died. Three are from my daughter who also died. They both died in 2003.

I have had eight children of my own and four are dead. One of my other sons is now very sick and can't walk. I think my husband is alive, but he left us a long time ago.

Life is difficult, but it is not my way to sit with my arms crossed.

I go to my small garden and work there, and I've also organized a little school where I look after other children during the day.

If people can, they give a little bit to help the school, but I don't ask anything of those who can't give. There are about 120 children at the school and about half of the children don't have parents, so they have nothing to give. It is the ones with parents who give a little to keep the school going. They will bring some food for all the kids, and other things we need.

It has been hard watching my grandchildren grow without their mother and father, but it doesn't make me angry. I do worry sometimes and I do get anxious about the future. But God gave me this. What can I do?

The grandchildren ask about their parents sometimes, and they have asked where they are and what happened to them. So we talk about them. They know their parents died, but they don't know they died of AIDS. Nobody really knows what they died of. They got sick, they got thin, and then they died.

I'm happiest when I look at my grandchildren when they are eating. I look at their faces and I can see where they have come from—that they are a part of me.

I can't possibly know what's going to happen in the future.

I worry about them contracting AIDS and I talk to the 14-year-old a lot about it.

If I had one wish now it would be to build a proper school so I can help other children while I'm helping my own.

Alice Cossa—sub-Saharan African grandmother

Quoted in *The Ottawa Citizen* © CanWest MediaWorks Publications Inc.

The Breath of God

Breathe little purple stem.
Breathe.
Your life lies before you.

Anxious thoughts we send control not your air.
Other hands manipulate, expectorate, irrigate.
Yet comes forth nothing.

Daddy whispers. Mama concentrates. Amma prays.
Time stands still.

But when the breath of God enters little purple stem,
Dear purple stem becomes blossom.
Blossom becomes Quinn Stephen Ronald.

And once again life begins,
Entirely dependent on the breath of God.

© Brenda Wood

I had no idea that a newborn baby was so purple, or that so much time could pass before it started to breathe on its own. I wrote this poem after witnessing my grandson's birth.

My Amazing Grandson

Who is this child with his dark curly hair and deep brown eyes? He came into the world after his four parents' mighty struggle. My daughter and her lesbian partner wanted him beyond expressing. His daddy and his papa were also overjoyed with his presence.

He lives in an alternate family but is deeply loved by his parents. He embraces the world of French day care, and his friends in the Beaches. He shines when his mama comes in and plays with his mummy. He loves to see his daddy and his papa in Toronto or New York.

And what about grandma, his lesbian grandmother who has no biological connection?

She had to grapple with what that means and how to be respectful to his mama. His mummy challenged me on that of course; I am his grandma because she is his mummy. So I love him as my beautiful, strong, grandson who brings hope to the world.

© Marcia Perryman

Night Visitor

"Grandma, there's a bat in the kitchen," Jordan exclaims,
his voice riding high, like the winged thing circling above
our Scrabble game.
"Grandpa, Grandpa," he calls up the stairs, and me,
I feel fear and panic rise up out of a deep slumbering place
to smother my heart.

"Open the door," I demand, "and hold Daisy Dog too."
Standing, I swing my arms, trying to create waves in the air,
to drive it away.
Jordan opens the door, immediately closing it,
saying mosquitoes will come in, making no sense to me.
Meanwhile the little beast flies between us and
up the stairs.

"Wake up! Wake up!" I shout at Jim.
"There's a bat hanging on your curtain."
And there hangs a dark teardrop blob against the
creamy curtain beside the bed.
Like a comic actor, Jim shakes his head and fights the
covers entangling him,
Struggling to shake night from his eyes,
to understand my panic-captured voice.

We three run through the rooms, sometimes anticipating
and sometimes chasing the bat's wild flight:
up the back stairs, down the main stairs.
Daisy Dog growls and yips her joy and bewilderment
at the confusion.

And then the bat is between us and down
on the carpet in the hall.

Carefully, with glove-covered hands,
Jordan cradles the intruder.
In wonder he holds the tiny creature,
part mammal, part myth,
before releasing it into the cooling night air.

For hours and hours I lie in my bed,
eyes refusing to close,
mind unable to trust the bat had re-entered the
otherworld of outer night.

© Kathryn MacDonald

What the Grandchildren Helped Me to Know

We arrived safely after a 16-hour trip from Myrtle Beach, South Carolina to home in Ontario. It's amazing what one can observe from spending a week with the grandchildren.

Here are my observations:

1. Once they're "uncorked" at 4:00 a.m. to get an early start, there's no putting the stopper back in before 10:00 p.m.
2. It's wise to carry large zip-lock bags in the van in case someone gets carsick.
3. Five videos make 16 hours on the road fly by faster. (Video players in the van must have been invented by grandparents who travelled with grandchildren.)
4. No matter how many hours you've been at the beach, it's always sad to leave.
5. Hair washed in ocean water doesn't comb well.

6. Boogie boards are fun to ride in on the waves, but if you don't get up in time, you skin your knees on the ocean floor.

7. It is fun to be buried by your grandchildren under a pile of sand. Giggling and wiggling one's toes creates cracks in the sand and they have to keep repairing the pile.

8. Sand sticks much better when you're wearing sun block lotion.

9. With the amount of sand that's brought home every day in the van, it's surprising there's any left by the ocean.

10. Mini-golfing with two six-year-olds is not like real golfing.

11. Taking grandchildren shopping is like taking a fox on a tour of a chicken house.

12. If you take a few artful bites out of a slice of bologna, you can make it look like a happy face.

13. Riding a scooter down the sidewalk is also fun for grandmothers.

14. Visiting an aquarium where there are live sharks, jellyfish, stingrays, and hundreds of other kinds of sea animals is truly amazing.

15. If someone can't go out for ice cream cones and wants you to bring one back, it's not really a good idea on a very hot day.

16. You can plan a surprise birthday party for a seven-year-old with the help of four cousins without anyone snitching.

17. Playing the game of jacks with grandkids is seriously competitive and hilariously funny.

18. You can find license plates from 30 different states and two Canadian provinces while driving.

19. No matter how many books you read at bedtime, it's never enough.

20. A great bedtime game is, "Ask Oma a Hundred Questions." "How many brothers and sisters do you have?" "How did you meet Opa?" "What's it like to be old?" "Where did you go on your honeymoon?" (This can also be reversed and you can ask them about their fears, hopes, boyfriends, etc.)

© Fern Boldt

Only God Knows

I don't know how old I am. I am really old.

I'm so old that I have got grown grandchildren and now three great-grandchildren. I have had five children of my own, but three have died. I'm not sure how many grandchildren I have. I just know the seven because they live in my house. The mother and father of my great-grandchildren are both dead, but I don't know where the parents of the seven grandchildren who live with me are.

Aside from the children, I am alone.

There is a suffering that comes with raising children who do not even have enough clothes to wear. I have a small garden and grow cabbage, but the ground is not very fertile so it doesn't grow well.

The grandchildren and great-grandchildren are good to me and never disrespect me. When I tell them what to do, they accept it. The older kids even do some of the cooking, but it is me who sweeps the house.

I didn't think I would still be looking after children at my age, but only God knows what's going to happen to our lives. I feel alive because of the children who live with me, even though I have to look after them.

Isabel Pene—sub-Saharan African grandmother

Quoted in *The Ottawa Citizen* © CanWest MediaWorks Publications Inc

"Blue Willow" Tea Time

"Grandma, you pretend that you are Tina, our maid," Amanda says to me as we carefully set the floral-paper-covered cardboard box on the kitchen table. I lift the lid to reveal the priceless set of "blue willow" patterned dishes, all in miniature size. Little dinner plates, tiny cups and saucers, a cream and sugar, a teapot, a meat platter, and even a gravy boat complete the collection.

This set is at least 45 years old, received as a gift when I was a child. Mrs. Rollins, who gave it to me, was the richest lady in our little village; my mom had once kept house for her before marrying my dad. My grandmother, as well as many families of that era, had a set of blue willow dishes, adult size, of course. I was so happy to have been given a set just like Grandma's.

I have no recollection of ever playing with my prized dishes. I remember the box being put on a bottom shelf in the spare room's closet, along with boxes of Christmas decorations and other treasures and keepsakes. Many of these things were brought out as the season demanded, but never my dishes. Mom told me that these dishes were special and we would save them. I had another cheaper set that my friends and I used with our dolls.

The years passed too quickly and the box of dishes was eventually forgotten until I became a mother. When my daughter was three or four, Mom gave the box to me but, again, cautioned that these dishes were very breakable and there were probably very few sets like them. I'm sorry to say that, after allowing my daughter a cursory examination and one or two tea times, I, too, tucked them away. Being a working mom, my time was focused on the demanding, practical side of life rather than on tea parties with my daughter.

For several years now, I have been a happy grandmother and am pleased to tell that the set has been used so much that the box is shredding its seams. My granddaughters, Amanda and Jessica, along with their dolls, are the guests of honour.

"Tina, could I have a little sugar for my tea, please?" I am asked. I hurry to fulfill my duty as the maid.

"Would Madam care for a cookie?" I ask Jessica.

She smiles and takes one from the little tray I am holding, the cookie so big that it dwarfs the tiny blue willow plate on which she puts it.

"And don't forget Jenna," she says, putting a cookie on the little plate in front of her doll. "Tina, aren't you going to have some tea too?"

"Thank you. I would like that," I say as I fill the demitasse-sized cup. I sip from it slowly, in lady-like fashion.

The jovial drama continues until the girls decide that it is time for Tina to clear the table. Then the little dishes are washed and carefully put back into their box, ready for the next "social."

I regret that I did not make time to have this fun with my daughter. Isn't it wonderful that grandparenting allows us a second chance? It is so delightful to "be a kid again"!

© Heather Campbell

Not the Worst of the Worst

I am 62 and have seven grandchildren.

Four are orphans. The youngest of the four is seven and the eldest is 15. I take care of the four. They are my daughter's children, but both she and her husband are now dead.

My own husband passed away in 2003.

We have no electricity, so I get up early in the morning at about 4:15 and walk to work. It takes about half an hour to get there and I start work at five o'clock. I work at tilling the fields. We do it with a tool—by hand.

I finish at 2 p.m. and usually bring some small vegetables home. It's then I start to cook for the children. After we finish eating, I do some housework and then go and visit people—usually two people a day. It's a community service. I talk to people about their problems and try to find solutions. We don't stop visiting a person until we have solved their problem.

My grandchildren are good students and up to now they are passing their exams. The eldest one is in grade 8 now.

One of the hardest parts of my life is finding the money to send my grandchildren to school on the bus every morning.

I sometimes feel very bad and lie awake at night worrying about the coming days and wondering how I am going to solve our problems. My grandchildren walk home for 10 kilometres.

When we are hungry and there is no food, we can go to people who have some to lend and we can borrow for our meals. It's a loan, and in return, the children must help them work on their fields until the debt is paid. But at least they have something to eat.

I am happiest when I am in my house alone and it is quiet and nobody is coming to ask me for money I owe and the children are not causing problems for me outside.

It's hard for me, but I'm not the worst of the worst.

> Marta Joa Machaieie—sub-Saharan African
> grandmother

Quoted in *The Ottawa Citizen* © CanWest MediaWorks
Publications Inc

Next Time We'll Go by Camel

This Nana's never doing that again.

Rachel's getting married. Come West, family. So came the summons to the nuptials of my beloved niece, two provinces over.

And that's why my grandchildren—three beans, three and under—and their parents and I found ourselves in the state in which we found ourselves last summer.

My husband, delayed by a funeral, would come later. But even without him, I could feel people staring as we negotiated the airports. I'd have stared too, if I'd had time: One big man and two look-alike women lugging two fold-up strollers, two car seats, three tiny blond kids (one in a third car seat and two straining at leashes), two luggage carts piled high, and various and sundry hand baggage draped over our shoulders like Christmas garlands—all dropping thither and yon, including the children.

We moved through the crowds, resembling nothing as much as a flock of Israelites—without the camel. People parted like the Red Sea at our approach. "Goodness, you're a gang!" the stewardess said, as we boarded the first plane.

"You should see the one we left behind," I said. "He uses a walker!" Her eyes bulged.

After flying an hour and a half, the plane touched down for a mid-flight change of planes. I held Tabatha (not quite two, and still too young for her own seat), took her adorable face in my hands, and said, "Tabatha, look at my eyes."

The tyke's eyes—a tad glassy—swivelled in my direction. "You've been such a good girl. Nana's so proud of you." She gazed back with that rather swimmy look, opened her mouth and upchucked. She drenched herself and my entire lap. Then she did it again.

The plane had arrived only minutes before our connecting flight's departure. We had no time to change. Our stench trailing us, we de-boarded, dashed through the airport and made the second plane just in time.

But it came to be that Benjamin, the eldest bean, refused to board the second plane, and chose instead to take a tantrum at the threshold of its door.

His parents, carrying the hand baggage, the car seats, and six-month-old Baby Dinah, had moved ahead of us in line. The last I saw of them was my daughter's eyes as, hearing her son's wails, she craned her neck over the shoulder of a fellow passenger. "You're on your own, Mom," I read in their helpless depths. Then the plane swallowed her.

I stooped to deal with Benjamin, but just then Tabatha decided to opt out of the vacation entirely. Wrenching her hand from mine, she put her little body in reverse and headed up the down ramp, darting between the legs of incoming passengers.

With Benjamin (in full tantrum mode) safely immobile on the floor, I fired after her, caught her, charged back down, scooped up the screaming bean, and carried them both into the plane.

God knows why this Nana isn't doing that again. And this Nana knows why he arranged the Exodus for the days before airplanes.

© Kathleen Gibson

Creating Memories

There is no greater gift you can give your grandchildren, besides your love, time and attention, than memories. They will last long after you are gone.

Luckily, my father valued the importance of memories. I can call upon so many special moments and events from my own childhood. That is what I want most to pass on to the four beautiful, intelligent grandchildren who have enriched my life immeasurably.

Tiny yellow boots splashing in a puddle; my grandson climbing a tree with abandon and sitting on a branch smiling down at me; hugs around my waist; and those words we all long to hear—"I love you Nannie"—are examples of what swells my heart the most.

When you are raising your children, life can be extremely busy and hectic, especially in today's society. Wise parents put it all into perspective and realize their children won't stay young forever. In all the hustle and bustle, they ensure their children are their main priority.

As grandmothers, we have moved on from that demanding timeframe and enter into a much more relaxed time in our lives. What was rather stressful in our mothering days—like juice spilt on the carpet—now seems such a minor thing: "It's only a carpet. Let's go clean it up."

I am energized by these curious minds, and I marvel at their ability to forge their own paths, even though the children are only aged four to seven. I answer their questions simply and honestly. If I don't know the answer, I'll find it.

I've given each child a personal treasure box to keep their "treasures" all in one place. It's each one's private box, and no one can look into the box without being invited. To receive that invitation and be trusted to share the contents of this treasure trove is one of the nicest compliments my grandchildren have given me. It always opens up some wonderful conversations.

One day, a grandchild asked if I had a treasure box. I replied, "No." Immediately my grandchildren encouraged me to get one and set about sharing their treasures with me. I'm happy to open that box for all of you and share some of its contents: three seagull feathers gathered when we were strolling at the beach; a piece of wood gnawed from a tree by a local beaver, a felt Christmas ornament decorated with beads and sequins, my grandson's favourite bouncing marble ball, pretty rocks gathered by the girls while on a walk around the neighbourhood, and tiny pinecones to save for creating a craft.

There is also a Sponge Bob Square Pants card that says: "You make me feel all bubbly," signed by my grandson. There is more: a piece of pretty pink ribbon from my granddaughter's Easter basket, notes of numbers they learned how to add in school that day, lines of scribble on some special paper from a granddaughter who hadn't learned how to print, and a drawing of a chocolate chip muffin signed with hugs and kisses by my oldest granddaughter.

Having had a wonderful, challenging career as a military wife and mother, I've learned it's not the quantity of the time you spend with loved ones, but the quality. Make each day count. Don't waste a second. Hug your grandchildren one more time. Tell each one individually, "You make me feel all bubbly."

© Dianne Collier

Not That Kind of Grandmother

It's blazing hot, and I'm watering my garden, myself, my grandson. Flicking my water wand at anything that looks like a candidate for raisin-hood under the midsummer sun.

"On face!" tiny Benjamin Bean squeals, sticking his hand into the flow and tentatively splashing his cheeks— ripe peaches below a set of blueberry eyes.

Well, why not? "On Granana's face too! On hair! On neck! On leg! On dress!" Liquid prisms absorb the sun and steal its heat before lighting on me, cool as a glacial stream.

"Lord, that feels good."

Benjamin watches, looks down at his blue shorts, already streaked with garden dirt from his excavation efforts. Nevertheless, "Take shorts off, Nana!" he pleads. I help remove them; then, "On knees!" he announces thrusting his chubby leg into the flow.

Some of my acquaintances, when they became grand-mothers, stepped up their beauty routine. Botoxed. Took out a membership in the gym. Changed their makeup to the age-defying line. Mustered whatever aesthetic troops they could gather to help them combat the label they felt heralded dotage. Increased their professional activities as extra assurance against weathering.

They seem to manage all that and grandmothering too. But I'm not that kind of grandmother. I want to be a fat grandma who bakes cookies, I've always said. I never had a grandmother, but in my dreams she baked and wore love handles under voluminous aprons.

I haven't gotten around to baking cookies lately—but

the grandbeans don't mind the "flower" ones their grand-father buys—thin ginger snaps we all love. And I've modi-fied my opinion about love handles. They obstruct a good time, so I'm staying slim. Ish. But I've given up on makeup almost entirely, as well as on trying to maintain a constantly stylish coiffure. There'll be plenty of that at the other end of these early years, I'm sure.

For now, I'm not that kind of grandmother.

I'd rather my grandbabies look into eyes that don't become black smudges when I splash water on them on a blazing summer afternoon. And touch hair that smells slightly like Russian Borscht and doesn't crackle like a hay bale when their fingers paw through it.

I'm fortunate that my writing jobs allow flexibility. Almost any day I'd rather be blowing a silly tune on a grand-child's toes than playing Scrabble for money. So today, while working at home, I put words aside to cavort in the sprinkler with a chubby-cheeked child. I may do it again soon. I haven't missed a deadline yet.

Another deadline motivates me most: a compelling urge that has shuffled my priorities like so many cards—the realization that God has offered me a second opportunity to help sculpt the life and values of a few infinitely precious human beans. A narrow slice of time that evaporates like water-beads in the sun, but casts long shadows into eternity.

I'm taking it. Because I am, after all, that kind of grandmother.

© Kathleen Gibson

Dancing Shoes

It seems just yesterday that Matthew and Jami were born—twins—the first, and probably the only, grandchildren for two delighted sets of grandparents.

And now they are five. Over a year and a half ago, when they had just turned four, Jami was determined to be a ballerina, and, to encourage this artistic expression, her parents enrolled her in an Ottawa branch of the Canadian School of Dance. So that he would not feel left out, they found a boys' dance class entitled "Boys Make Noise" for Matthew.

It soon became apparent that Jami did not have the determination of a young Karen Kain. She began to rebel against the discipline of her hour-long class, and eventually dropped out. Matt, on the other hand, loved "Boys Make Noise," and, some months later, proudly invited us to his Spring Recital.

Four grandparents, Jami, and her dad, crowded into the packed auditorium while his mom took Matthew with his costume to join his class backstage. The jeans, the plaid shirt, the kerchief, and the miniature Stetson were in the bag, but, oh-dear-me, the boots for the cowboy dancer had somehow been left at home!

"Never mind," Matthew announced, "I'll just wear my crocs."

Sure enough, when Group #27 trotted onto the stage, there was one especially cute cowboy sporting a Stetson at a jaunty angle, and on his feet, a pair of orange crocs. The cowboys danced up a dust storm, swinging their lariats and galloping around the stage like a pack of semi-trained horses, when suddenly, there was a flash of orange flying towards the audience.

Out of the line charged our mini-cowboy. He felled the flying footwear, and he cantered back into place. The audience burst into loud applause. Our Matt was, to us at least, the star of the show!

Sad to say, as a result of circumstances beyond his control, Matthew was unable to continue "Making a Noise" this year, but that did not mean he stopped dancing. And neither did Jami. Recently, all eight of us were at a wedding, and for a time after dinner, the children joined the adults on the dance floor.

The bride was a step dancer, and at one point, the music changed to an Irish jig. Soon we were aware that most of the crowd had stopped dancing to encircle one small dancer, clapping as they watched. Her large brown eyes flashing, her dark hair swirling, her feet flying in perfect time to the lively music, our erstwhile ballerina had become an Irish dancer—a dancer who had abandoned her pinching party shoes in favour of her comfortable pink crocs!

Riverdance, here they come! (Or so one proud grannie is allowed to imagine.)

© Charlotte McWilliam

Grand!

Roses…crumbling, brown, wilt on a windowsill,
love forgotten!
Silent, but begging to be heard!

He fell hard for a seventeen-year-old girl,
Her head full of dreams, so pretty and sparkly…
she broke men's hearts!
While her mother, tears in her own once-pretty eyes,
buys a t-shirt at a garage sale that reads,
"Grandmas are just antique little girls! "

The day before she finds out from her youngest son that
her oldest son
has not gotten around to telling her yet, that she is soon to
become—
A grandma!
She grumpily stands in front of the stove making a bologna
cup with a
fried egg in it, like her grandma taught her to…
She waves her plastic spatula like it is an award for being
wholesome,
then, in terrycloth slippers and faded robe she stands on
the front
porch, elated and shouts
"Yes!" to a could-care-less world!

© Pamela Hunt

first published in her book, *Antique Roses*

Grandmothers' Necklace

Sometimes, I Don't Have an Answer

I am 58 and I have three grandchildren aged 12, six and four who live with me.

They are my daughter's children. The eldest of my own seven children is 36 and the youngest, the mother of my grandchildren, is 23.

My husband died from cancer when my eldest child was 11 years old.

All of my seven children are still alive, but the father of my grandchildren—my son-in-law—is dead and their mother is very sick.

So I am looking after my sick daughter and my grandchildren, but all my children are still with me except the 36-year-old.

I don't know exactly what illness my daughter has, but she is getting very slim—slim, slim and slimmer all the time.

I don't suppose anybody really knows what is the matter.

I make a little money from being a member of community organizations and helping other people.

I also had a little field where I plant some cereal we can eat and sometimes I can sell. I can also work in fields for other people who pay me a little.

We help each other when we are in need. I don't have much, but when I look around, I can see people who are worse off than me.

"Grandma, what are we going to eat?" the children ask. Sometimes, I don't have an answer.

Leia William Mabunda—sub-Saharan African grandmother

Quoted in *The Ottawa Citizen* © CanWest Media Works Publications Inc

Necessary Havoc

When Corrie comes to my house
And I the door unlatch,
My first thought is — forgive me
"Batten down the hatch!"

She's like a sudden summer storm,
No warning or no clue.
She strikes just like a hurricane;
Everything's askew!

First, it is the kitchen, garbage, drawers
She swoops and swirls and spins
And twirls and wheels and pirouettes,
Then stops and slyly grins.

A whirlwind spinning round and round,
Then down the hall she flies.
She bursts upon the bathroom
Where multi "NO"s she spies.

Then out the door and to my room
Not losing any power,
She wreaks her mischief fully.
This is her finest hour!
An unleashed force of nature,
An energy unbound —
She's seeking to discover
What makes the world go 'round.

But Mom and Dad and Grandma
Are patient, for we know
That Corrie's curiosity's
The thing that makes her grow.

© Erma Johnson

bue ~ Abuela ~ Lita ~ Ajji ~ Baba ~ Babka ~ Babcia ~
Maw ~ Bamma ~ Go-Go ~ Bana ~ Banma ~ Beebaw ~ Bibi
ig Gram ~ Big Mama ~ MeMot ~ Mim ~ Bubbie ~ Bubbles ~
Ma ~ Cici ~ Mommom ~ Da Ma ~ Lola ~ Ma ~ Maga
Mai ~ Mama ~ Mamaw ~ Mamie ~ Mammo ~ Mams ~ Maw-
~ Mardi ~ Marme ~ Mema ~ Meme ~ Grand-Mère ~ Memog
Memom ~ Mica ~ Mima ~ Moggee ~ Moggy ~ Momaw ~
mers ~ Mom-Mom ~ Moome ~ Nai Nai ~ Mummica ~ Mum
na ~ E-li-si ~ E-ma ~ Eena-nana ~ G-Mom ~ Nanny ~ GaGa ~
s ~ Gammie ~ NeeNee ~ Gammlemor ~ Gammy ~ Gigia
nie ~ Gee ~ Ge-Ge ~ GiGi ~ Gommie ~ Gommy ~ Grama ~ Mor-
~ Na'nah ~ Namaw ~ Namma ~ Nan ~ Nana ~ G-Ma
agrandma ~ Nanoo ~ Naunua ~ Nema ~ Ni Ni ~ Ninna
ny ~ Nona ~ Nonna ~ Nonnie ~ Nonno ~ Nonny ~ Nun Nun ~
achan ~ Oma ~ Gogo ~ Pabby ~ Gram ~ Grammie ~
mmommie ~ Gramms ~ Gran ~ Gran Gran ~ Grandma ~
ndmama ~ Grandneir ~ Grandmomma ~ Seanmhathair ~
nma ~ Granmomma ~ Granny ~ Grannymama ~ GreatMother ~
Yia ~ Gumma ~ Kupuna wahine ~ Baachan ~ Grannie ~ Pama
ia-Yia ~ Gramma ~ Gramsy ~ Grams ~ Phar-Mor ~ Grandnan
randmom ~ Grandmother ~ Sasa ~ Granna ~ Slo-ma ~ Sweetie
weetums ~ Tetah ~ Tutu wahine ~ Vo-Vo ~ Lela ~ Nanna ~
gie ~ Grand-mère ~ Abue ~ Abuela ~ Lita ~ Ajji ~ Baba ~
bka ~ Babcia ~ MeeMaw ~ Bamma ~ Go-Go ~ Bana ~ Banma ~
Beebaw ~ Bibi ~ Big Gram ~ Big Mama ~ MeMot ~ Mim ~
bbie ~ Bubbles ~ Mo Ma ~ Cici ~ Mommom ~ Da Ma ~ Lola ~
~ Maga ~ MaiMai ~ Mama ~ Mamaw ~ Mamie ~ Mammo ~
ms ~ Maw-Maw ~ Mardi ~ Marme ~ Mema ~ Meme ~ Grand-
re ~ Memog ~ Memom ~ Mica ~ Mima ~ Moggee ~ Moggy ~
maw ~ Mommers ~ Mom-Mom ~ Moome ~ Nai Nai ~ Mummica
Mum ~ Nanna ~ E-li-si ~ E-ma ~ Eena-nana ~ G-Mom ~ Nanny
GaGa ~ Gams ~ Gammie ~ NeeNee ~ Gammlemor ~ Gammy ~
ia ~ Gannie ~ Gee ~ Ge-Ge ~ GiGi ~ Gommie ~ Gommy ~ Grama
Mor-Mor ~ Na'nah ~ Namaw ~ Namma ~ Nan ~ Nana ~ G-Ma
Nanagrandma ~ Nanoo ~ Naunua ~ Nema ~ Ni Ni ~ Ninna ~
ny ~ Nona ~ Nonna ~ Nonnie ~ Nonno ~ Nonny ~ Nun Nun ~
aachan ~ Oma ~ Gogo ~ Pabby ~ Gram ~ Grammie ~
mmommie ~ Gramms ~ Gran ~ Gran Gran ~ Grandma ~ Grand

~ Abue ~ Abuela ~ Lita ~ Ajji ~ Baba ~ Babka ~ Babci MeeMaw ~ Bamma ~ Go-Go ~ Bana ~ Banma ~ Beebaw ~ G ~ Big Gram ~ Big Mama ~ MeMot ~ Mim ~ Bubbie ~ Bubbl Mo Ma ~ Cici ~ Mommom ~ Da Ma ~ Lola ~ Ma ~ Mag MaiMai ~ Mama ~ Mamaw ~ Mamie ~ Mammo ~ Mams ~ M Maw ~ Mardi ~ Marme ~ Mema ~ Meme ~ Grand-Mère ~ Mer ~ Memom ~ Mica ~ Mima ~ Moggee ~ Moggy ~ Momaw Mommers ~ Mom-Mom ~ Moome ~ Nai Nai ~ Mummica ~ Mu Nanna ~ E-li-si ~ E-ma ~ Eena-nana ~ G-Mom ~ Nanny ~ GaG Gams ~ Gammie ~ NeeNee ~ Gammlemor ~ Gammy ~ Gigi Gannie ~ Gee ~ Ge-Ge ~ GiGi ~ Gommie ~ Gommy ~ Grama ~ M Mor ~ Na'nah ~ Namaw ~ Namma ~ Nan ~ Nana ~ G-M Nanagrandma ~ Nanoo ~ Nuunua ~ Nema ~ NiNi ~ Ninne Ninny ~ Nona ~ Nonna ~Nonnie ~ Nonno ~ Nonny ~ Nun Nu Obaachan ~ Oma ~ Gogo ~ Pabby ~ Gram ~ Grammie Grammommie ~ Gramms ~ Gran ~ Gran Gran ~ Grandma Grandmama ~ Grandmeir ~ Grandmomma ~ Seanmhathair Granna ~ Granmomma ~Granny ~ Grannymama ~ GreatMothe YaYa ~ Gumma ~ Kupuna wahine ~ Baachan ~ Grannie ~ Pa ~ Yia-Yia ~ Gramma ~ Gramsy ~ Grams ~ Phar-Mor ~ Grand ~ Grandmom ~ Grandmother ~ Sasa ~ Granna ~ Slo-ma ~ Swe ~ Sweetums ~ Tetah ~ Tutu wahine ~ Vo-Vo ~ Lela ~ Nanne Bougie ~ Grand-mère ~ Abue ~ Abuela ~ Lita ~ Ajji ~ Babe Babka ~ Babcia ~ MeeMaw ~ Bamma ~ Go-Go ~ Bana ~ Ban ~ Beebaw ~ Bibi ~ Big Gram ~ Big Mama ~ MeMot ~ Mim Bubbie ~ Bubbles ~ Mo Ma ~ Cici ~ Mommom ~ Da Ma ~ Lol Ma ~ Maga ~ MaiMai ~ Mama ~ Mamaw ~ Mamie ~ Mamme Mams ~ Maw-Maw ~ Mardi ~ Marme ~ Mema ~ Meme ~ Gran Mère ~ Memog ~ Memom ~ Mica ~ Mima ~ Moggee ~ Moggy Momaw ~ Mommers ~ Mom-Mom ~ Moome ~ Nai Nai ~ Mumm ~ Mum ~ Nanna ~ E-li-si ~ E-ma ~ Eena-nana ~ G-Mom ~ Nan ~ GaGa ~ Gams ~ Gammie ~ NeeNee ~ Gammlemor ~ Gammy Gigia ~ Gannie ~ Gee ~ Ge-Ge ~ GiGi ~ Gommie ~ Gommy ~ Gra ~ Mor-Mor ~ Na'nah ~ Namaw ~ Namma ~ Nan ~ Nana ~ G- ~ Nanagrandma ~ Nanoo ~ Nuunua ~ Nema ~ NiNi ~ Ninne Ninny ~ Nona ~ Nonna ~Nonnie ~ Nonno ~ Nonny ~ Nun Nu Obaachan ~ Oma ~ Gogo ~ Pabby ~ Gram ~ Grammie Grammommie ~ Gramms ~ Gran ~ Gran Gran ~ Grandma ~ Gra

part three

Intergenerational Relationships and Aging

"I endure their intimacy
the slow movement of their heads
as they turn to one another
and then simultaneously look down
into the rolling baby's nest —

"into the eyes
of the flesh they share.

"…and the ache inside me
wants to know —
if they know
how lucky they are."

© Linda Patchett, from "The Lucky Ones"

Two Friends

Two friends.
At least they could have been
Had it been written in the plan.
One, an octogenarian;
The other, not yet a man.

Both—outrageous,
Slightly thunderous,
Competitive to a fault!
She was known for candour,
He, as a great sport.

The jokes they'd tell…
About themselves!
A gift that's all too rare.
Guffawing at their own mistakes
Their laughter filled the air.

Two friends.
At least they could have been
Had it been written in the plan.
She, an octogenarian;
He, not yet a man.

© C.G. Mordaunt

The Lucky Ones

I watch them daily

padding the sidewalks
with effortless strides –
grandmother and daughter taking turns
at the helm of the baby stroller.

The trio
a perfect three-leaf clover.

Like fresh puffed pastry
their sated cheeks rise up
with words that jiggle.

Ripe with laughter their warm mouths
click incessantly—
in sync
with the wind's breath.

I endure their intimacy
the slow movement of their heads
as they turn to one another
and then simultaneously look down
into the rolling baby's nest—

into the eyes
of the flesh they share.

The infant—
the blossoming sun-flower of their attention
the three of them together—
unbroken
under the same bounteous sky

and the ache inside me
wants to know—

if they know
how lucky they are?

© Linda Patchett

Echoes and Innocence

A Selection of Haiku

I
lush green lawn—
together an old couple
push the mower

II
orthopedic clinic—
the skeleton watches
leaves

III
another funeral
once we went
to cocktail parties

IV
Christmas card list—
so many names
crossed out

V
mall mannequin
nearly blind mother says
"He's smiling at me"

VI
once the old teacher
was proud of her writing—
I try to read it

VII
old tombstone
my grandchild's mitten
touches praying hands

© Winona Baker

I: from new collection, *Nature Here is Half Japanese* II: orthopedic clinic HI #40, 2000; ANTH *Poems From The Basement.* Leaf Press Can 2002, III: *Moonset* Edition 4 #2, IV, V: HI #53 Japan 03, VI: *Frogpond #* XXX111 USA, *Haiku Friends* –Japan, VII: Anthology *Haiku Friends* 11 –Japan

Grandma's Golden Pitcher

As far back as I can remember, Grandma's golden pitcher sparkled behind the etched glass of her china cabinet. Its dimpled surface reflected light. Grandma had inherited the metallic gold pottery from her grandmother. In my childhood, its contents—milk or lemonade—always flowed, as did Grandma's wisdom. "Love and light," she'd often say, instead of hello or good-bye. Now the pitcher sits atop my bookshelf, reminding me of Grandma.

After Grandma died, I moved to San Diego. One early morning before going to work, I watched the rising sun over the eastern Cuyamaca Mountains outside my front window. Dawn flamed the sky orange as clouds formed and reformed. One golden cloud looked like Grandma's pitcher spilling sunlight onto the landscape. Then I heard Grandma's voice: "Pour love into your work and light into your life, Shinan." I closed my eyes and imagined love-light streaming into my apartment, even onto the recently smashed Volkswagen Bug sitting in my driveway.

A few weeks earlier, I'd failed to stop at the throughway. Another driver had plowed into the VW, crunching both cars. Luckily, no one was injured. The accident was my fault.

The body shop man had shaken his head as he submitted his estimate for repairs to my uninsured VW. "Two thousand, but it isn't worth fixing." I had neither the money nor a credit card. Paying the rent was a struggle. So, I prayed for a miracle.

Two days later, a Hispanic man knocked at my door. "I fix your car. Make good deal."

Who sent him? I felt Grandma's presence and heard her voice, "Pour love into this family." What family? I wondered.

"Five hundred dollars," the dark haired man said.

I wanted to jump at the offer, yet was afraid of a scam. "How will you work?"

"Here. I have tools. See." He lifted the toolbox he was carrying. "I am Manuel Vargas. Twenty years experience." He paused, scuffing the toe of his boot on the cement steps. "Now, no job." He pointed to a beat-up Pinto parked at the curb. "Kids need food." I stared at the faces of a woman and four children. Were they living in the car?

"I have food. I'll borrow money." We bargained—$300 and most of my canned food.

Manuel was pounding out the fender with a rubber mallet as I went inside to make ten peanut butter sandwiches and stir up two quarts of lemonade. I took the food and drink to the car. "Aqui," I said to the woman. She nodded. I noticed her tear-stained face. "Habla usted Ingles?" She shook her head, then reached in the back seat for a boy's hand.

"Raimundo!"

"I have English," he said shyly.

"Here are sandwiches and lemonade." I handed the paper bags through the window. "There's a park three blocks up this street with a drinking fountain, a sand box, swings and a bathroom. You could walk there with your mother and play while your dad works on my car."

The boy translated my words.

"Sí! Sí!" the children shouted.

"Gracias," the mother smiled.

Manuel spent the day soldering, sanding, puttying and

welding. I watched in amazement as he used a portable acetylene torch. I cleared my cupboards and bagged up food, then called friends for money. By evening, I'd come up with three hundred dollars and, to my amazement, Manuel had smoothed out the fender, bumper, chrome and door.

"Needs paint," he patted the car door, pleased with his work. "Trabajo de amor." A labour of love.

"Sí," I smiled. "Gracias!" We shook hands, happy with our exchange. I watched Manuel drive off. The children waved. As I turned to go back inside, light from the setting sun enveloped the Volkswagen.

"Thank you, Grandma," I whispered. Back inside my apartment, Grandmother's pitcher glowed in that setting sun.

© Shinan Barclay

Have Patience

Have patience with my fury.
Sometimes, awareness
Creeps into my mind,
Boldly taunting, mocking my weaknesses,
Darkly unwelcome
Cruel reminders
Of someone I once was, and am no more.

Have patience when I'm fearful.
Alone, in darkness,
I hear Death's whisper
Calling, summoning my unwilling soul.
By day, surrounded,
Overwhelmed, I cringe
From threatening sound and blurring motion.

Have patience; I'm forgetful.
Daily dull routines
Form vague memories.
Your name escapes on blowing winds of time.
Early years, relived—
Young, handsome, loved—
I bask in health and immortality.

Have patience when I'm fretful.
Unsure, halting steps
Betray me, prompting
A jealous guard of substance in my grasp.
Rejecting by force

Soft tasteless foods,
I spit, and hurl offending bowl in spite.

Have patience with my frailty—
Aged bones grown brittle,
Eyes dimmed, hearing dulled.
With petty fretting tantrums, frustrations
Mirror my losses.
Have patience now—
You, too, may one day walk the path I'm on.

© Joyce Gero

The Presence of Yia-Yia

I.

my dear boy:
thus began the message; I could have waited until you
called; I chose not to do so;

the pause here was brief but heavy; like an ocean; heavy;

so, you found your way into my dreams last night;
I don't read anything into such things; to be honest;
but I figure I should check up on you;

her voice sparkled and lifted me.

© Theodore Christou

II.

She is accustomed to my absence
She said do
not
Permit
yourself to fail
I trust in your abilities
She said
You cannot fail
She said
Do well in
all of your endeavours

She is accustomed
To my absence
She is not much prone to tears
She wakes and
Giggles at the morning
She and I have different cares

© Theodore Christou

III.

Did you keep the flower?
Of course I kept the
flower. You gave it to me.
My hearing is great. It
hurts a little only on
windy days like today.
I'm waiting for my CT
scan results to come in
next week for my final prognosis,
so please, fingers crossed.
I think I'll recover fully and live
to tell about it. One thing
is for certain: the world is
more beautiful when you
can listen clearly to
beautiful music (even
the horrible sounds of traffic).
Thank you for the
concern.

© Theodore Christou

Visitation

The painkillers
scrambling her brain, or maybe
a dream. She knows all the logical explanations why,
on the night after her baby came
too soon, the night after she'd laboured
for nothing, knowing she must push,
push, like the doctor
said, knowing
that the child
she was urging out
was unready
to be born,
her grandmother appeared
at the foot of her hospital bed
with a small pink-blanketed form cradled
in her arms,
Whispering, don't worry, darlin',
I'll care for her until you can be here.
Whispering, don't you worry none, sweetheart,
you won't have to come for years and years, but
when you do this moment will seem
like yesterday, like none of us have ever
been apart. Then she blew a kiss
and disappeared.

Her grandmother,
eight years dead, standing
in that sterile white room
offering comfort, love
a promise of eternity.

© Ronnie R. Brown

"Visitation" previously appeared in *Night Echoes*, by Ronnie R.
Brown, Black Moss Press, 2006.

Grandmothers' Necklace

Two Wise Women

When I was young
gazing into my grandmother's eyes
I saw a wild child at play
usually clad in smudged crinoline gowns
or ripened rummage-sale dresses
with musical notes of plums and olives
leaping past ankles that would bite into
the plush mulch of her sprouting bouquet
Like an enchanted butterfly floating
in a field festival of forget-me-nots
her mind would dazzle and dash
and then alight on the touched side of things
And now that her earth-dance is over
I see that she was a sage woman—
the wisest I have ever known
Son,
today you think I am mad—

The Root Woman who collects feathers for her flower
basket—pitching plump mantras at the moon—
or lingering in the thrumming of a waterfall that crests
a still-thirsty womb—
One who inhales fire and water
through the crusty pads of naked feet
while lying scar-side up
unpolished
on the dirt floor of sweat lodges

But when I have crossed over
into the inner circle
connecting beginning to end
you will feel the depth of my longing
and you will know the truth
in the breath of these words

Your heart eyes will open on spirit wings
and I too,
will be seen as a wise woman
like my grandmother before me

Son—
Be hungry, too

© Linda Patchett

No Exceptions

Clara Bolt wasn't sure, when her husband Frank advised her to take it easy driving to the eye doctor—was he being sarcastic? Clara prided herself on her driving. As she often told her grandchildren, "I obey the law to the letter."

She checked in at nine for her 9:15 appointment. Nobody was ahead of her. By the time she had put down her glasses and health card, four people had lined up behind her.

The lady at the desk put drops into Clara's eyes and took her to an adjoining room. Clara climbed up on a stool in front of a miniature gallows. She pressed her head against the noose to find green dots on a monitor and record them by pressing a button. It was a tiring exercise. A bell rang and no more dots appeared, but Clara persevered until the nurse returned.

"Sorry to have kept you waiting. That office is jammed and the phone rings, rings, rings. Let me adjust you for the other eye."

When she returned to the waiting room, Clara was surprised to find it crowded.

She put on her jacket and headed for the door. "That performance didn't do much for my eyesight!" she muttered. In the hall she found it hard to control her footsteps. Perhaps if she were to sit down and read for a bit, everything would return to normal. Not a chair, let alone a magazine, could she find.

Disoriented, Clara went to the car thinking of all the things she could be doing at home. Fresh air might help; she rolled down the window. Finally, she had enough of waiting and backed up very slowly. She inched the car to the exit and waited until there wasn't a car in sight in either direction before turning right.

It was so difficult to get things into perspective that she didn't notice a dog. She heard a yap and some man yelling, "What are you trying to do? Kill my dog?"

It was upsetting to see so many cars coming toward her even though they were in the opposite lane. They blurred by too fast and seemed to slew a bit. She'd best go ahead on the green light, rather than make a right turn. At the very intersection she most dreaded, a man on a bicycle to her right wobbled about as if he were drunk.

Frank was mixing compost in the driveway in front of the garage when she arrived. She parked outside.

"Did I ever have a time getting home!"

"Is it the drops?" Frank asked.

"I've had them before and always managed all right."

"You didn't get into any trouble?" Frank sounded apprehensive.

"Of course not!"

The phone rang and Frank went in ahead of Clara to answer it.

Clara put her glasses on the hall table and removed her jacket. No place like home. Things were normal already.

Frank handed her the phone. "It's for you—the eye people."

Something must be awfully wrong with her eyes! The nurse had said they wouldn't call if all was well; if anything were wrong, she'd be called within a week.

"Mrs. Bolt, have you your right glasses?"

"Of course."

"Look at them, please. Are they bifocals?"

Clara picked up the glasses. They weren't bifocal. Their frames were the same size, but they were brown and hers were silver.

"I'm afraid they aren't mine."

"No, they belong to a lady who is still here. Could you bring them over?"

"Oh, I can't. I could hardly drive home."

"That's because you had the wrong glasses."

"What's up?" Frank asked.

When she explained, Frank shook his head. "St. Christopher must be on duty...driving with someone else's glasses! When you knew something was wrong, why didn't you take them off?"

"I didn't know they weren't mine. Besides, if you need glasses to drive, you are obliged to wear them."

© Jean Turnbull Elford

Mom-Mom's Irish Soda Bread

Yesterday I baked Irish Soda Bread. I imagine I've baked a hundred or more loaves of it over the years. I believe I could close my eyes and make it without even thinking, but I never do. When the mood strikes me, the first thing I do is search out the tattered piece of paper on which my grandmother scratched down the recipe.

I gingerly unfolded the recipe and set it on the counter. After all these years, it is now yellowed with age and generously perfumed with the scent of caraway. The telltale sprinkling of smudges from spices and other traces that have accidentally fallen onto the page over time only add to its character. Like a well-worn flag, this ragged slip of paper bears proudly the scars of its long and happy life.

As I read it over yesterday and gathered the ingredients together, my mind drifted back to the stories I know by heart of how she and Pop-Pop met on the boat to America from County Cork, Ireland. I pictured her chestnut brown hair and blue eyes, the same hair and eyes I see when I look in the mirror.

I'm sure Mom-Mom didn't need a recipe to bake the soda bread. She learned how to make it from her mother, as I learned how to make it from mine. Most likely she jotted the recipe down on a piece of paper so that some little bit of her would be left behind in this world, to pass from one generation to the next. So it went on to my mother, and is now among my treasures where it will stay until it's my turn to pass it on. It may be a long wait. As of right now, I can't imagine parting with it.

The preparation ritual continued as I gathered the ingredients and began to mix the dough. Over the years I've adapted the recipe to suit a modern-day kitchen, but the spirit with which I bake is centuries old. The essence of our Irish Soda Bread is the lilt in my grandmother's voice and the light in my mother's eyes. This little scrap of paper I hold so dear awakened memories in me that can never be erased. What could warm a grandmother's heart more than that? Perhaps this was her intention all along.

As the bread baked, the aroma filled the air. I was transported back in time. I breathed in deeply and imagined myself as a schoolgirl once again, standing at my mother's side, learning the process of mixing the dough. Mom had a way of turning kitchen chores into a special kind of fun. Never once did she ban me from experimenting to my heart's content in the kitchen.

The minor recipe adjustments I've made have no great effect on the outcome. The finished product is delicious every time. To my way of thinking, it always tastes better to the keeper of the recipe than it does to anyone else.

The secret to enjoying the bread is the knowledge that you have the knack to make it come out just right. Not because the recipe is perfect; it's not. The spirit in the baking is. It's hard to spoil the taste of childhood memories. The love of my mother and grandmother has assured their sweet preservation.

© Annemarie B. Tait

The Journey of the Dresses

The girls play dress-up
with grandmother's castaway clothing

Strapless bonnets, veiled and feathered hats
for church-goers only
they dally like plumed ostriches
their toes tipped in floppy, spiked heels

They learn to fall—to get back up
to reclaim themselves over and over again

Puffed in bunting bag dresses
and wrapped in beaded necklaces
gracefully dangling between twigged knees
they squeal like two little seals

They promenade in front of their granny
as she dubs them her "little hooligans"
and offers up the final touch—
a smidgen of rouge to each tiny cheekbone

The gentle kneading of her thumbs
tickling more laughter into the room

Draped in the innocence of white crinoline
they romp in childhood gaiety—
grand hosts of a lavish tea party
they step out into the yard to cross entire continents

Grandmothers' Necklace

Reeling their way into other imaginary worlds

Later the dresses are washed
in anticipation of tomorrow's adventures
hung-out-to-dry they flap wildly
sparring with the wind

Two middle-aged women silently press
the creases on a few limp dresses
the dancer, no longer in them

They pack thin-worn blouses and stretchy slacks
a safety pin still attached
where a polished button once glistened

The sisters mourn their grandmother's final sunset—
forever golden

They caress the crinkles on the once white crinoline
now yellowed and tattered around the edges

They hang the dresses and patiently wait
for granddaughters

To travel into them

© Linda Patchett

Daisy Chain

"You think of me as *which* kind of flower, Robert?"

"A daisy."

"Not a velvety rose or dainty violet? A daisy is a common, stinky, dusty, roadside weed!" Though my choice of words may give me away, I'm trying to *sound* calm. This event, our marriage preparation course, does, after all, indicate our chances of success in marriage, and I'd really like it to work.

"Why a daisy?"

My discomfited fiancé, Robert, tries to explain his choice. "Because," he stammers, flinching before my thundercloud face, "you are bright and *usually* cheerful, and you are strong. *Yes*—a daisy."

That scene took place some time ago. The story was in the making long before then. Though Robert and I were both unaware of this, the narrative began with my grandmother.

Both of my grandmothers died long before I was born. I received my maternal grandmother's filigree brooch when I was a young teen. It had a diamond chip in the centre and a tiny ruby on each side. I loved that brooch but lost it. Devastation!

In my parents' bedroom, my mother and I used to look at the possessions she stored in her cedar "hope" chest. I loved hearing Mom tell her treasures' stories. The unusual floor-length pale-green wedding dress with countless covered buttons and the elegant silver strap shoes I knew about. Someday, they would be mine. The snowflake pieces crocheted by Mom's grandmother would also be passed on to children, grandchildren and great-grandchildren. Items actually handled or, better still, created by my foremothers, meant a lot to me.

As a young teenager, I discovered a new prize. It was a shallow wooden box, its outside painted with black enamel, its inside, scarlet. The lid was a slightly larger separate piece that fitted neatly over the box. On the surface glowed a hand-painted bouquet of white daisies and a tiny Monarch butterfly, both gilded. On the underside of the box's bottom was painted a double "E" for Emily Eliza, my maternal grandmother. Mom said this container had held fine handkerchiefs. The belief was that my grandfather, a commercial artist and letterer, had painted the box. It was then that I discovered my reputedly vivacious grand-mother's nickname—"Daisy."

I had never told my husband about the box. In fact, I'd forgotten all about it until I was cleaning out my mother's home, many years after that premarital discussion.

There is one more link I haven't mentioned—a neck-lace, a one-inch diameter circular flat glass pendant sus-pended on a gold chain. When an ornamental top screw is turned sufficiently to be removed, the circular frame springs open, releasing two glass circles and whatever has been placed between them. Once, the pendant held pic-tures of my great-grandmother and great-grandfather, one on each side. I've saved the pictures but the pendant now holds the symbol of my continuing connection with my mother's side—a pressed daisy. For some special occasions, I am "traditional" and wear the pendant with a frilly old-fashioned blouse.

After more than thirty-five years of marriage, with five children and five grandchildren in the mix, I've had time to review.

"I'm a daisy? I am a daisy, and proud of it. How did you know? Thank you, Robert!"

© Patricia Anne Elford

Playing Scrabble At Midnight

in sleep, my grandmother is there
coaxing me to play at midnight

I tell her it's late, but run to get my new glasses
she doesn't know that I need them to read now

she sifts through smooth, sand-glazed tiles
thick black letters etched into the wood

sometimes, she creates words
that only she and I can grasp

absent from the dictionary
these are the precious words we cling to

she nudges pieces of tile
across the table

I spot an I_1 and a V_4
as she unites them with the R_1 of another word

to spell
RIVER

it is where I know I will find her—
in the river of tears gathering

on a vacant triple word score, or meandering
in the ancient river of dreams

I wake up—unsure of what message
the letters have massaged into my bones

I wait in the darkness
for the next visit

the next word

© Linda Patchett

Apology

"I'm sorry I loved him,"
was all she said
like blue sky lightning.
But this was a misdirected apology.
I was a generation removed
from those childhoods lost
to life-scarring indignities:
(Un)forgotten stillborn siblings
buried in the backyard,
Foul rats prowling bedrooms
for young exposed flesh.

"It's okay. You did your best,"
I half chided in response
like a faulty electric blanket.
I had no right to this conversation;
it belonged to others
We arrived at the bus station.
I helped her climb aboard
knowing that this journey home
would at last be restful and that
she would not pass this way again.

© Matthew Reesor

The apology my grandmother gave me, quite unexpectedly, the last time we saw each other, was a monumental moment of repentance and forgiveness seeking. Perhaps it eased a burden of responsibility she'd carried, raising eight children in an environment marked by abject poverty and child abuse inflicted by my grandfather. My father, oldest of eight, occasionally shared some of his childhood's darker realities with my sister and me. My grandmother's brave apology was an encouraging final gesture of profound love for her family.

My Grandmother's Voice

Look for me
by the river
where I watched you from our kitchen window
as you swam or skated in rhythm with the seasons

Look for me
in the vacant gaps along the treetops
and in the sated patches underneath
in the mystery light of the moon
and in the shadow that entices darkness

Look for me
in the summer haze of burning fields
in the thrill of a mid-winter's storm
in the hot and cold thrusts
of ever turning suns

Look for me
in the tall, unruly weeds that sway
and in the still, short stubble of cropped grass
in the cracked bark of an aging oak tree
and in the polished grain of a miniscule seed

Listen for me
in the sleepy trickle of the creek
as it snuggles up against the rocks
    Listen, and you will hear me calling your name
in the raucous caw of the crow
in the crooning lull of the loon

and in the soothing pipe of the sparrow
    the way I always did when you were little
    and needed reminding

Look for me
in the winged footprints of your three sons
in the coming birth of new passages
and in the passing down of old stories

Look for me
in the gentle breeze
for I am the wind's chaste breath
gracefully sweeping warm kisses
across your face

Look—and you will find me—

Meet me in the circle where our lives began
on the water's edge and we will begin again

My granddaughter, my friend

© Linda Patchett

Round

All the cookies of my girlhood were round,
those that Grandma made from rolled-out dough
cut with a glass and dusted with glistening sugar;
those made by my Mom and dropped with a spoon
onto the shiny cookie sheets,
raisins and nuts peaking out through the batter.
Cookies were served on round plates,
stored in round tins.
Round is the shape of my girlhood,
round as a hug.

© Kathryn MacDonald

My Granny, My Gem, Kathe Jans

I don't believe my grandmother ever lost her patience when people mispronounced her name. Kathe Jans served fourteen years in public life, so she would have had to remind people on more than one occasion that her first name was pronounced "Katy", not "Kathy". She was the first woman elected as Deputy Reeve in Innisfil (near Barrie, Ontario), where she had spent years as a school board trustee and city councillor. Kathe was also an active member of the federal Liberals. Leading party figures—including Prime Minister Pierre Elliott Trudeau—knew her by name.

I was named after this remarkable woman, my granny. She loomed larger than life to me when I was a child. She was always an inspiring role model: a female leader who worked for the betterment of her community and her country.

Kathe Jans was born Katharina Gauder in November 1924, in Krnjaja, Serbia (then Yugoslavia). In 1941, having only been able to complete a Grade 5 education, she began working for a Jewish family. When Germany invaded Yugoslavia she was arrested, then detained in German labour camps for years until liberated by American forces. In the fall of 1945, as a refugee, she received her first food parcel from a Canadian agency, with a note signed by future Prime Minister Lester B. Pearson. Her father and stepmother, already living in Canada, were relieved to finally locate her in Europe.

Kathe immigrated to Canada in 1948, having long con-

Grandmothers' Necklace

sidered this country as her salvation. Two years later, she married my grandfather, Joe Jans—whom she met in Toronto, but who was born Josef Janzekovich in Ptuj, Slovenia—and gave birth to my mother, their only child, in 1953.

While many European immigrants who came to Canada after World War II share similar stories of adversity, my grandmother continued to struggle as a champion for democracy and human rights. She is remembered as outspoken and opinionated, but with tremendous compassion and generosity of spirit. She believed there was no room for prejudice. She was driven by her own personal edict of "love thy neighbour". Kathe never took for granted the freedom and opportunity she had been given when she became a Canadian citizen. She was a proud supporter of public education; my visits to her house as a child would always begin by our reviewing my latest report card or school assignment. She encouraged me to write, and she helped teach me how to live with an open heart.

Recently I discovered a scrapbook my grandfather had made of Kathe's press clippings and election campaign flyers. Because her campaign slogan was always "Kathe Cares", I think that her death on Valentine's Day in 1991 was poetic. I was only eleven when she passed away, but I feel closer to her now than ever before.

I wish she had been there to celebrate my accomplishments in high school, or to commemorate my graduation from the University of Toronto, when I became the first woman in our family to finish university. I also wish she could have lived to be part of the work that I've done since then—mobilizing young people to vote, lobbying the government, advocating for an end to global poverty, and raising awareness about inequities in access to HIV/AIDS medications.

Although I didn't know it at the time, my granny had a tremendous influence on my understanding of the change that one person can make. In recent years, I recognize the ways in which her values have become mine. I will continue to live more closely by her example, and do so proudly— even as I occasionally have to correct the pronunciation of my name.

© Kathe Rogers

Contributors

Here are the generous men and women, of varied backgrounds, now living in Canada, the United States and Ireland, who answered the call to share their gifts to help the heroic daily efforts of grandmothers in sub-Saharan Africa.

Winona Baker, a Haiku specialist from British Columbia, received the top global prize in a 1989 World Haiku Contest. Winona's work appears in her own books and over 70 anthologies in North America, New Zealand, Japan and Europe; including *The Haiku World: An International Poetry Almanac*. Poems have been translated into Japanese, French, Greek, Croatian, Romanian, and Yugoslavian. See www.abcbookworld.com

Eileen Barber. Born in Grandview, Manitoba. Lived in Winnipeg, Toronto and Petawawa, Ontario, Doerlinbach Germany and Brunssum Netherlands, and now in Pembroke, Ontario. Her most outstanding achievement—raising three children who are independent and considerate. Most enjoyable job—helping to start, and working in, the Petawawa Public Library. Latest job—volunteering.

Shinan Barclay, M.A., is a writing coach, storyteller and the co-author of *Rainmaker's Prayers, The Sedona Vortex Experience* and *Moontime for Kory,* a Puberty Rite-of-Passage. Her work has been translated into five languages and appears in numerous anthologies. A ceramic artist, she lives on the Oregon Coast. www.facebook.com/shinanbarclay; www.moontimeforkory.blogspot.com; www.shinanbarclay.author.blogspot.com

Glynis Belec, as a freelance writer, author and private tutor, has been happily writing for twenty years and has a particular passion to write for and about children. She has had two children's books, plays, short stories and over 1000 magazine articles, newspaper columns, plays and devotions published. gbelec@everus.ca, www.inscribe.org/glynisbelec, http://glynis-myjourney.blogspot.com

Chantal Bigras, whose degree is in Special Needs Education, was born in St-Jerome, PQ. She was a coordinator for the BC and Yukon Heart and Stroke Foundation. She and husband Danis Laverdure live in Petawawa, ON, with sons Marc Antoine and Olivier. For language students, Chantal developed a study technique which uses colours.

Fern Boldt, a graduate of Tyndale Seminary in Toronto, is a counsellor, ESL teacher, golfer, scrap-booker, editor and writer. Some mice in her extensive collection have become characters in her children's books. Married to author Peter Boldt, she is the mother of four married sons and "Oma" to nine grandchildren. http://fernboldt.wordpress.com

Rose Brandon, from Sault Ste Marie and Manitoulin Island, Canada, a graduate of Master's College, has authored many published essays, articles and devotionals, as well as Shirley Brown's biography, *Vanished*. She writes and teaches Bible and small group studies, and co-writes financial articles with husband Doug. Rose speaks at churches, conferences and retreats. http://rosebrandon.com/index.html

Ronnie R. Brown is an Ottawa writer whose work has appeared in over one hundred magazines and anthologies including: *Arc, Valum, The Fiddlehead,* and *Event.* Following her four previous books of poetry, her fifth, *Night Echoes* **(Black Moss Press, 2006)** was short-listed for **The Acorn-Plantos People's Poetry Award**, an honour which her fourth collection, *States of Matter* (Black Moss, 2005) won in 2006.

Frances Burton, retired from the University of Toronto, is grandmother of phenomenal children: two boys and a girl from phenomenal twin daughters. Born in France, she has lived in Canada with her journalist husband since graduating from CUNY in Anthropology. Her most recent book, *Fire: the Spark that Ignited Human Evolution,* is now published.

Phil Callaway, speaker, and daddy of three, is a best-selling, award-winning author of twenty-four books. Phil has been called "the funniest Canadian alive", never by his school teachers. He's a frequent guest on national radio and TV. His humorous family life stories feature in hundreds of magazines worldwide. His *greatest* achievement was convincing his wife to marry him. Phil lives in Alberta, Canada with his high school sweetheart. They're married. callaway@prairie.ed / www.laughagain.org.

Heather Campbell, Beachburg, Ontario, Canada, retired in 1996 after 35 years of teaching. A member of the Ottawa Chapter of Canadian Authors' Association, she has had three books of memoirs published. Mother, grandmother, piano teacher, organist and writer, Heather, with husband Frank, also loves to travel. Learn more at www.hfcamp.com

Priscilla Carr's poetry appears in *Northern New England Review, INSPIRIT,* and *It Has Come to This: Poets of The Great Mother Conference.* Her uplifting memoir vignettes appear in Adams Media's *Cup of Comfort and Hero Series.* Donald Hall and Robert Bly are her mentors. Richie, her husband, is her Ever Muse.

Bella Mahaya Carter is the author of SECRETS OF MY SEX. Her poetry, fiction, and creative nonfiction have appeared in *The Sun, Onthebus, Calyx, Pearl, Literary Mama* and elsewhere. Bella teaches classes, and works as an editorial consultant and writing coach. She lives in Southern California. Visit her online at www.bellamahayacarter.com.

Theodore Christou is Assistant Professor of Education at the University of New Brunswick. His academic and fictional writing explore philosophical and historical themes. A Canadian of Greek-Cypriot heritage, Theodore's poetry largely concerns reconciliation of cultural, geographical, and linguistic divides. http://www.unbf.ca/education/faculty/christou.html

Cheryl (Lowther) Coates, the first girl born one year in Springhill, Nova Scotia, has long enjoyed playing with words. Continuing an interrupted education, she graduated in the top quarter of New Brunswick adults. A military wife, mother of three, and grandmother-wannabe, Cheryl's been active in organizations beneficial to women and children.

Dianne Collier is a military wife, mother, grandmother, author, columnist, and founding member of CFB Petawawa's Military Family Resource Centre's Board of Directors. Dianne received awards for her wholehearted, creative support of military spouses. Her wry book, *Hurry Up & Wait*, was a Canadian bestseller, followed by *My Love, My Life*. http://www.renc.igs.net/~tcollier/index.html "Seagull Selections"

Dianna Robin Dennis, writer and composer, lives on a farm near Galway, Ireland. Her non-fiction horse books have been translated into many languages. Her poems and essays have appeared on Irish radio and in print world-wide. Her blonde hair will soon crave blue highlights. Often neglected website: www.diannarobindennis.com. See: MySpace.com.

Grandmothers' Necklace

J. Graham Ducker, a retired teacher, author and poet, in 2008 was invited to deliver a key-note address based on his book *Don't Wake The Teacher!* at the International WEFLA Education Conference in Cuba. First place winner of the Lichen Epistolary Fiction 2006 and the Mariposa Writers' Group Short Story Competition 2008. www.grahamducker.com

Terri Elders has reminisced for *Chicken Soup for the Soul, Cup of Comfort,* and *Mature Living.* She, her husband, Ken Wilson, dogs and cats live near Colville, WA. A public member of the Washington State Medical Quality Assurance Commission, she received the 2006 UCLA Alumni Association Community Service Award for her Peace Corps and VISTA work.

Jean Turnbull Elford, following her extra-mural Western University B.A., began freelancing. Her first submission appeared in The *Canadian Geographical Journal.* Others followed in farm papers, newspapers and magazines. One was read on the CBC. Jean authored *A History of Lambton County* and *Canada West's Last Frontier,* Lambton County Historical Society books.

Patricia Anne Elford, B.A., M.Div., is an educator, clergy person, and award-winning professional writer, in various *genres,* published in literary publications, periodicals, anthologies, and on line. She edits shorter pieces and books, including this anthology—a fundraiser for **Grandmothers to Grandmothers**. Inspired, Patricia writes on anything "handy", including her hands. Bogged blog: www.stillwatersanddancingwings. blogspot.com

Gillian Federico, mother of six, ages 12 to 36, and grandmother of six, as a Chaplain for the Canadian Forces, longs for the time she used to have to knit. Her husband still proudly wears an Arran sweater she knitted for him when they were courting over 38 years ago. gillianandpaul.federico@sympatico.ca

Joyce Gero, of Atlantic Canada, has been writing since childhood, working in various forms and genres. Recently published work includes a contribution to a 2006 Nimbus anthology, *Christmas in the Maritimes.* Joyce is currently employed at a federal correctional facility, where she formerly volunteered as a creative writing course teacher.

Kathleen and **Rick Gibson** live in Saskatchewan, Canada, very near their grandbeans. Veteran writer, speaker, and columnist, Kathleen is author of *West Nile Diary, One Couple's Triumph Over A Deadly Disease* (2009) and Word Alive non-fiction winner for *Practice by Practice* (2009). Access Kathleen's weekly faith and life column, "Sunny Side Up": www.kathleengibson.ca

Martha Deborah Hall has degrees from Ohio Wesleyan and Columbia University. Her *Abandoned Gardens* won the 2005 John and Miriam Morris Chapbook contest. In 2009 Plain View Press published the following books of Hall's poetry: *Two Grains in Time* and *My Side of the Street.*

Sandy L. Hazell lives with her husband in Markham, ON. They are blessed with two adult children. Sandy has many years of writing experience for both mainstream and Christian media; most recently, she has enjoyed writing personal experience and non-fiction creative stories.

Kat Heckenbach is a freelance writer and aspiring novelist, with personal essays appearing in Sunday School periodicals and short fiction published in several online magazines. A graduate of the University of Tampa, she is also an artist and home-schooling mom. Enter her

world at www.findingangel.com
or www.kat-findingangel.blogspot.com.

Pamela Hunt, a "country girl" who loves
the city, was first published at age 17 in
Sassy Magazine. She's had six children.
Betwixt raising children, she sold her
articles to magazines. She has also sold
three books. Pamela, her two grandsons
and two cats live harmoniously in her
lakeside cabin.

Ruth Zaryski Jackson was born in Toronto.
She studied Anthropology, worked in
research, teaching and heritage
planning. After raising three children,
she writes memoir and poetry. In 2008,
her story *Room in My Heart* was
published in *The Wisdom of Old Souls.* A
charter member of Life Writers Ink,
Ruth lives in Mount Albert.
Email: rzaryskijackson@gmail.com,
www.memoirwritersworld.blogspot.com

Erma (Bennett) Johnson was born in
Forester's Falls, Ontario, educated in
R.R. #6 Ross, Cobden District High,
Ottawa Teachers' College and Ottawa
University (English/ Philosophy degree).
An elementary school teacher, Erma
most often taught grades 7 and 8. Her
hobbies include gardening, writing,
golfing, and entertaining with singing
and guitar.

Heather Kendall is the author of a *Tale of Two Kingdoms*. She has published articles in *The Canadian Gideon, The Fellowship LINK, Faith Today* and *Daily Devotions for Writers*. She is also on the editorial committee of *The Fellowship LINK*. Heather lives in Innisfil, Ontario. www.tale2k.com www.tale2k.blogspot.com

Tracie Klaehn is a psychotherapist in Kitchener. She lives with her husband, three daughters, and golden retriever Hubble. She has a passion for reading, writing, playing flute, kayaking, and the outdoors.

Marcia Lee Laycock's inspirational writing has won awards in both Canada and the U.S. Her devotionals are distributed to thousands and her novel, *One Smooth Stone*, won the Best New Canadian Christian Author Award in 2006. Marcia is a sought-after speaker at women's events. Visit her at www.vinemarc.com

Janet LaPlante writes from her beliefs of how we grow though human experience, authoring a column "Joy from Janet". She freelances for newspapers and magazines and is finishing her book "My Children's Children." Janet is married with four children and three grandchildren and is an active member in her community.

Kathryn MacDonald, B.A, M.P.A., transforms stones into amulets, has worked at *Harrowsmith* and *Equinox* magazines, been a ghostwriter, editor, workshop leader, article and essay writer. Her poetry has appears in literary journals such as *Descant*, *The Fiddlehead*, and *Northward Journal, Ascent Aspirations* magazine. Kathryn's novel, ***Calla & Édourd*** was launched recently. *See:* http://sites. google.com/site/jewelleryartisan/ Photo by Darren MacDonald.

Judy Maddren's voice has been familiar to millions of Canadians as the host of CBC Radio's World Report. Judy is now, with Alannah Campbell, recording **Soundportraits**, autobiographical interviews. The memoirs become treasured family keepsakes. Judy lives with her husband Tim Elliott in Toronto. They have four children. www.soundportraits.ca.

Charlotte McWilliam is a former high school teacher who has discovered the joy (*and frustrations*) of writing in her retirement. She and her husband divide their time between Deep River, travelling, and their beloved cottage. She is an active *Deep River Granny* and a proud mother and grandmother.

Ruth Smith Meyer's life has provided many beads for her memory necklace. Since the death of her husband of thirty-nine years and remarriage to a childhood friend, she mothers a combined family of eight adult children and spouses and eighteen grandchildren. She enjoys writing and speaking about her life. **www.ruthsmithmeyer.com**

C.G. Mordaunt started writing songs as a teenager. She has written plays, skits, and a children's musical, all of which have been performed publicly. She studied creative writing at the University of Toronto and is a graduate of the Institute of Children's Literature. She and her husband live in Toronto.

Mary Anne K. Moran is an author, keynote speaker, and Nutritional Educator. Her experience in the Natural Health Industry spans more than twenty-five years, and the release of her book, *"Before I Knew You Loved Me"* has made her a much sought- after speaker for conferences and events. Website: mak-moran.com

Theodore Oisin is a writer from Kitchener, Ontario. Her story, "Letter to Granny Zora" took place when she was thirty years old, before she left her homeland.

Jean Ostrom retired after careers in several fields, including teaching, scientific research and project management. She immediately opened a bed and breakfast with her husband of 40 years, and enjoys hosting guests from all parts of the world. She heads the Petawawa Grannies, raising funds for AIDS-ravaged families in Africa.

Linda Patchett — *"She enters the pond, Swims among the frogs—Anything—to hear her own voice."* A teacher. Loves: three amazing sons, a Big Bear with the gentle spirit of a lamb, and *Three Suns*, their home. A dog lover—She lives with her cat Ollie. Favourite poet—Mary Oliver.

Jacinthe Payant is the youngest child of nine. She has raised two children as a single parent and has worked most of her life with children and high risk families. She now supports women who have been victims of sexual assault. As she suffers from a degenerative disc disease, writing books and poetry help her to deal with her own suffering.

Marcia Perryman: English immigrant, happy grandmother of three, was raised in Deep River. She and her husband taught in Newfoundland. She completed her M.Ed. in Ontario. Founder of an Orillia battered women's shelter, Marcia practised family therapy in Barrie, Mississauga, and Pembroke. She was a Metropolitan Community Church minister. A separation and breast cancer changed her life.

Linda Dawn Pettigrew has had many lives. Currently an active grandmother, and a developing writer who teaches ESL and literacy in Toronto, she's written, edited and published articles, essays and educational resources, over the past decade. *My Grandmas, A & P* is the first publication of her autobiographical work.

June Powell's fondest memories are of summers spent on her grandparents' farm in the B.C. Interior. There Granny encouraged her to play Grandpa's fiddle when he was not looking! June lives with her husband, three cats and a dog who likes music. She is writing her first children's book.

Matthew Reesor is a writer of poetry and short fiction from Kingston, Ontario. He often collaborates with his sister, Sarah Reesor, a visual artist and painter living in Granville Ferry, Nova Scotia. Matthew lives with his wife Nina and young sons Jacob and Elijah.

Ann Ritter, a South Carolina native, has made her home in the Atlanta area for 30 years. A writer, performer and business woman, whose areas of expertise are communication planning, and personal healing through storytelling and movement, Ms. Ritter practises as a yoga therapist and teacher of yoga and meditation.

Kathe Rogers has extensive experience in communications, fundraising and advocacy, and has collaborated on various editorial projects and special events. She currently works at Dignitas International, a medical humanitarian HIV/AIDS organization, and volunteers with the Ontario Association of Food Banks and RESULTS Canada. Kathe is frequently a moderator, public speaker and guest lecturer.

Dr. David C. Schwartz, *Professor Emeritus of Public Health, Rutgers, New Jersey, Professor of Medicine at the Miller School of Medicine, U. of Miami,* lives with his wife, Paula in Aventura, Florida. Author of five books and 50 scholarly articles on public policy, he now concentrates on spiritual and children's literature.

Alison Seay writes full-time as many different people. Once in a while she even writes as herself. This poem is one of those instances. More about Alison's work can be found at Kamikaze Writer (http://www.alisonseay.wordpress.com).

L. June Stevenson is an award-winning author and editor. For 24 years she was editor of *Glad Tidings* magazine with The Presbyterian Church in Canada. Her published works include poems, articles, meditations, worship services, and hundreds of greeting card verses in both denominational and secular publications across North America.

Melanie Stiles is an award-winning freelance poet, poetry judge, and writer of regular columns whose writing, arising from her personal faith-challenging experiences, appears in many anthologies, in newsletters, and on the web.

She is a life coach, author and speaker, active in Lakewood Church, Houston, Texas. http://melaniestiles.com

Ray Succre, who lives on the Oregon coast with his wife and son, is a widely published poet. His novels in print are *Tatterdemalion* (2008) and *Amphisbaena* (2009), (both published through Cauliay). A third, *A Fine Young Day*, is forthcoming in Summer 2010. He tries hard. Publication History: http://raysuccre.blogspot.com, Book Releases and Journal: http://raysuccre2.blogspot.com

Michael J. Sullivan, a graduate of many entry level jobs, beginning in the New York Stock Exchange, wrote his earliest poem, "A Bum", in 1999. Earlier military duty in South Korea prompted "Blue and Gray" (DMZ) and "Carry On" (recovery). His thirty years with the railroad didn't inspire any poetry.

Denis Taillefer's work has been published in various on-line and print magazines, and he has won awards for his work. He says he is honoured to be participating in this project.

Annmarie B. Tait resides in Conshohocken, PA with her husband Joe and Sammy the "Wonder Yorkie". In addition to writing stories about her large Irish Catholic family and the memories they made, Annmarie also enjoys singing and recording Irish and American Folk Songs. Contact Annmarie at: irishbloom@aol.com.

Carolyn Wilker is a writer, editor, speaker and storyteller from Kitchener, Ontario. Writing credits include articles, op-ed, devotionals, book reviews and poetry. Her poetry has been published in *Voices and Visions, Vol. 6, Writers Undercover, vol. x; Tickled by Thunder, Tower Poetry, Esprit,* and *Glad Tidings.* Website: www.carolynwilker.call

Mary Ann Wilson is a freelance writer and editor who lives in southern Ontario with her partner-in-all, Neil. Besides coloured glass beads, things that make her smile include vanilla ice cream, properly-used apostrophes, and the beach of her childhood along the North Channel of Lake Huron.

Brenda Wood, a Canadian, is a conference speaker and author specializing in common sense solutions for the Christian life. Her latest book is "Heartfelt, 366 Devotions for Common Sense Living." Contact Brenda at: brendawoodauthor@yahoo.ca www.size10hopefil.wordpress.com

Abue ~ Abuela ~ Lita ~ Ajji ~ Baba ~ Babka ~ Babca ~
e Maw ~ Bamma ~ Go-Go ~ Bana ~ Banma ~ Beebaw ~ Bibi
Big Gram ~ Big Mama ~ Me Mot ~ Mim ~ Bubbie ~ Bubbles
Ma ~ Cici ~ Mommom ~ Da Ma ~ Lola ~ Ma ~ Maga
Mai ~ Mama ~ Mamaw ~ Mamie ~ Mammo ~ Mams ~ Maw-
w ~ Mardi ~ Marme ~ Mema ~ Meme ~ Grand-Mère ~ Memog
Memom ~ Mica ~ Mima ~ Moggee ~ Moggy ~ Momaw ~
mmers ~ Mom-Mom ~ Moome ~ Nai Nai ~ Mummica ~ Mum
nna ~ E-li-si ~ E-ma ~ Eena-nana ~ G-Mom ~ Nanny ~ GaGa
ms ~ Gammie ~ Nee Nee ~ Gammlemor ~ Gammy ~ Gigia ~
nnie ~ Gee ~ Ge-Ge ~ GiGi ~ Gommie ~ Gommy ~ Grama ~ Mor-
or ~ Na'nah ~ Namaw ~ Namma ~ Nan ~ Nana ~ G-Ma ~
anagrandma ~ Nanoo ~ Naunua ~ Nema ~ Ni Ni ~ Ninna ~
nny ~ Nona ~ Nonna ~ Nonnie ~ Nonno ~ Nonny ~ Nun Nun ~
baachan ~ Oma ~ Gogo ~ Pabby ~ Gram ~ Grammie ~
ammommie ~ Gramms ~ Gran ~ Gran Gran ~ Grandma ~
andmama ~ Grandmeir ~ Grandmomma ~ Seanmhathair ~
anma ~ Granmomma ~ Granny ~ Grannymama ~ Great Mother ~
a Ya ~ Gumma ~ Kupuna wahine ~ Baachan ~ Grannie ~ Pama
Yia-Yia ~ Gramma ~ Gramsy ~ Grams ~ Phar-Mor ~ Grandnan
Grandmom ~ Grandmother ~ Sasa ~ Granna ~ Slo-ma ~ Sweetie
Sweetums ~ Tetah ~ Tutu wahine ~ Vo-Vo ~ Lela ~ Nanna ~
ougie ~ Grand-mère ~ Abue ~ Abuela ~ Lita ~ Ajji ~ Baba ~
abka ~ Babcia ~ Mee Maw ~ Bamma ~ Go-Go ~ Bana ~ Banma ~
Beebaw ~ Bibi ~ Big Gram ~ Big Mama ~ Me Mot ~ Mim ~
ubbie ~ Bubbles ~ Mo Ma ~ Cici ~ Mommom ~ Da Ma ~ Lola ~
a ~ Maga ~ Mai Mai ~ Mama ~ Mamaw ~ Mamie ~ Mammo ~
ams ~ Maw-Maw ~ Mardi ~ Marme ~ Mema ~ Meme ~ Grand-
ère ~ Memog ~ Memom ~ Mica ~ Mima ~ Moggee ~ Moggy ~
omaw ~ Mommers ~ Mom-Mom ~ Moome ~ Nai Nai ~ Mummica
Mum ~ Nanna ~ E-li-si ~ E-ma ~ Eena-nana ~ G-Mom ~ Nanny
GaGa ~ Gams ~ Gammie ~ Nee Nee ~ Gammlemor ~ Gammy ~
igia ~ Gannie ~ Gee ~ Ge-Ge ~ GiGi ~ Gommie ~ Gommy ~ Grama
Mor-Mor ~ Na'nah ~ Namaw ~ Namma ~ Nan ~ Nana ~ G-Ma
Nanagrandma ~ Nanoo ~ Naunua ~ Nema ~ Ni Ni ~ Ninna ~
inny ~ Nona ~ Nonna ~ Nonnie ~ Nonno ~ Nonny ~ Nun Nun ~
baachan ~ Oma ~ Gogo ~ Pabby ~ Gram ~ Grammie ~
rammommie ~ Gramms ~ Gran ~ Gran Gran ~ Grandma ~ Grana